Bill Donovan
105 Lance Ct
Santa Cruz, CA
408-459-6594

HÀNYǓ

FOR BEGINNING STUDENTS

• PETER CHANG • ALYCE MACKERRAS • YU HSIU-CHING •

STUDENT'S BOOK

LONGMAN

Addison Wesley Longman Australia Pty Limited
95 Coventry Street
South Melbourne 3205 Australia

Offices in Sydney, Brisbane and Perth,
and associated companies throughout the world.

First published 1992
Reprinted 1993, 1994 (twice), 1995 (twice), 1996 (twice), 1997

Designed by Sylvia Witte
Illustrated by Yang Qiulin
Cover photo by William Thomas
Set in 10/11pt Helvetica (English and Pinyin) and
Simplified Kaisho (Chinese characters)
by Graphicraft Typesetters Ltd, Hong Kong
Produced by Addison Wesley Longman Australia Pty Ltd
Printed in Malaysia through Longman Malaysia, CLP

National Library of Australia
Cataloguing-in-Publication data

Chang, Peter.
Hànyǔ for beginning students. Student's book.

ISBN 0 582 87003 8. (Australia)
ISBN 0-88727-221-5 (USA)

1. Chinese language –Textbooks for foreign speakers – English.
2. Chinese language – Problems, exercises, etc. I. Mackerras, Alyce.
II. Yu, Hsiu-ching. III. Title.

495. 182421

Distributed in the United States and Canada by
Cheng & Tsui Company Inc.,
25 West Street,
Boston MA 02111 - 1268, USA

The publisher's policy is to use **paper manufactured from sustainable forests**

CONTENTS

ACKNOWLEDGEMENTS

The revision of the first volumes of the *Hànyǔ* series, of which *Hànyǔ for Beginning Students* represents the first stage, has been made possible by a grant from the Asian Studies Council and the authors would like to thank the Council for its support. We would also like to thank the Key Centre for Asian Languages and Studies, Division of Asian and International Studies, Griffith University and particularly its director, Professor Colin Mackerras, for the use of facilities and continued support for this project.

We would also like to thank the many teachers and students whose practical experience has contributed to the shape of the revisions. We would particularly like to thank Ms Chui Lee of The Southport School, Southport, who has been a principal consultant on the *Hànyǔ* course.

We especially want to thank Ms Yin Guiqin, of the Beijing Language Institute, who read the manuscript of *Hànyǔ for Beginning Students* and made many valuable comments and also Professor Huang Zhengcheng, also of the Beijing Language Institute, who generously made himself available for endless discussions on, often seemingly inscrutable, points of grammar and usage.

INTRODUCTION

Recent decades have seen growth in the study of Asian languages in Australia, reflecting the growing awareness of the importance of Asia in our cultural, economic and political life. The study of Chinese has been part of this growth, with Modern Standard Chinese being officially designated one of the 'languages of wider teaching' having significance to Australia for external and economic considerations as well as being an important community language within Australia itself.

The *Hànyǔ* series has been compiled in response to the need for Chinese language teaching materials suitable for Australian secondary students. The seeding funding for the series came from the Australia-China Council, which was set up by the Federal Government in 1979 to promote understanding between Australia and China. The first volume, *Hànyǔ 1*, was published in 1985, *Hànyǔ 2* was published in 1986 and *Hànyǔ 3* in 1990.

Hànyǔ for Beginning Students represents the first stage in the revised editions of the first two volumes, *Hànyǔ 1* and *Hànyǔ 2* of the *Hànyǔ* series. These revisions reflect the changing emphases in language teaching in Australia and are also a response to the practical needs of teachers and students in our schools. The revisions are made possible by a grant from the Asian Studies Council.

The topics covered in *Hànyǔ for Beginning Students* have been selected as ones which will enable students to use the Chinese language communicatively in their immediate environment, such as the classroom. Language items such as grammar and structures have been kept to a minimum, while at the same time there is an increased number of activities and exercises designed to consolidate or expand material learned. The right-hand column in the *Student's Book* contains exercises and suggestions for communicative activities, while the *Practice Book* contains exercises involving both communicative activities and practice exercises in listening, speaking, reading and writing.

A major revision is that the unit texts are written in characters from the very beginning. *Hanyu pinyin* is also used to facilitate the learning of pronunciation and recognition of characters, as is consistent with standard practice in Chinese texts for beginners in the language. It is dropped once the characters have been targeted for learning through their appearance in the Learn to Read or Learn to Write character sections.

The *Student's Book* is the basic volume for the *Hànyǔ for Beginning Students* course. It comprises four units, each designed around a topic or general area of communicative activity. Around this general topic, the unit provides a variety of language items through a series of dialogues which serve as models of communicative language use and which in turn are supported by suggested activities, exercises, grammar explanations and cultural notes. Units are sub-divided into areas, each of which focus on a specific aspect of the communicative activity. For example, where the general area of communicative activity of the unit is talking about one's family, the unit will be divided into areas such as describing who is in one's family, talking about pets or expressing age. Each unit also contains a Learn to Read section and is followed by a Learn to Write lesson in both of which the texts are written exclusively in characters. The characters used in these texts are those which students are expected to learn either to recognise or to write.

A key feature of the *Hànyǔ* material is the integration of all aspects of the course and of the four macro skills of listening, speaking, reading and writing. The main texts in the units are the source from which come all the vocabulary items, characters, functions and notions, grammar and cultural information which together form the content of the course. All activities and exercises and the Learn to Read sections and Learn to Write lessons relate to these texts so that the various elements of the course are fully integrated and serve to reinforce one another.

Hànyǔ for Beginning Students is accompanied by cassette tapes which contain recordings of all texts, listening exercises (in both the *Student's Book* and the *Practice Book*) and the texts from the Learn to Read sections and Learn to Write lessons.

The *Teacher's Book* contains a comprehensive explanation of the methodology used in the course. It also sets out in detail the sequence of items as they occur in the *Student's Book* and the *Practice Book*, thus making clear the relationship between the two. The *Teacher's Book* also contains more detailed notes on grammar and usage for teachers' reference, the texts of all listening exercises and the solutions to all puzzles and word games contained in the *Practice Book*.

When the revisions of the first two volumes of the *Hànyǔ* series are completed, the revised course will be as follows:

Hànyǔ for Beginning Students (based on *Hànyǔ 1*)
Hànyǔ for Intermediate Students Stage 1 (based on *Hànyǔ 1* & *2*)
Hànyǔ for Intermediate Students Stage 2 (based on *Hànyǔ 2*)
Hànyǔ for Intermediate Students Stage 3 (present *Hànyǔ 3*)
Hànyǔ for Senior Students (still in planning stage)

UNIT 1 Hello!

第一单元

Dì-yī dānyuán

你好！

Nǐ hǎo!

In this unit you will learn something about China and the Chinese language. You will also learn how to greet your friends and say goodbye to them, and how to identify yourself and say what country you come from.

1.1 中国 – 汉语 Zhōngguó – Hànyǔ

Zhōngguó and Hànyǔ

China is a vast land, third largest in area after Russia and Canada and possessing the largest population of any country in the world. The civilisation of China is one of the world's oldest living civilisations. Its written language, existing records of which date back to over 3000 years ago, has a far longer history than any other writing system in use today.

In traditional times, the Chinese believed their country was a unique land of civilisation surrounded on all sides by 'barbarians'. Therefore, their country became known as *Zhōngguó* (中国), literally 'The Central Kingdom'.

What is usually referred to as Chinese is, in fact, the language of China's largest nationality, the Han. (*Hànyǔ* (汉语) literally means 'the language of the Han'.) In the past, the people of 'The Central Kingdom' were known as 'the people of Han' and this was the name given to one of China's earliest and greatest dynasties, the Han Dynasty, which lasted from 206 BC to AD 220. Today, the people of the Han nationality make up over 92 per cent of China's total population.

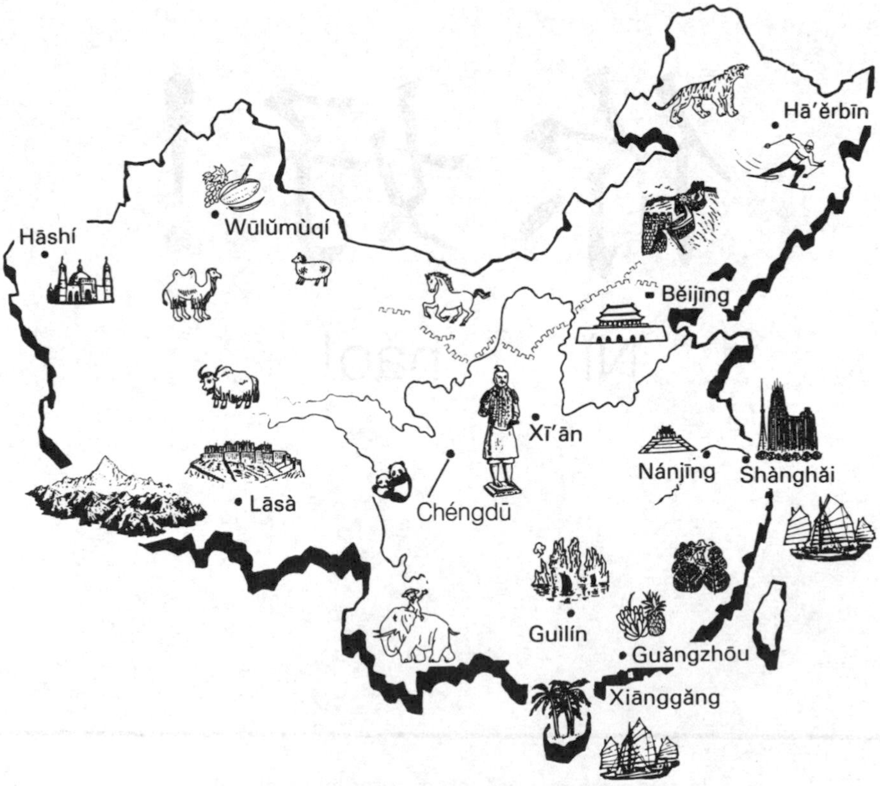

Apart from the Han, there are over fifty other nationalities in China. These minority nationalities constitute only 6.7 per cent of the total population, but they occupy about 60 per cent of China's total land area, much of it in the western regions of China and China's borderlands. Minority nationalities possess their own distinct culture, their own language and often their own writing system.

The Uighurs live in Xinjiang in the west of China. They are a Turkic people, culturally quite distinct from the Han Chinese. Most Uighurs are followers of the Islamic faith.

The Mongolians live on the plains of Inner Mongolia. They are mainly a pastoral people and excellent horseriders. Many Mongolians live in the traditional yurt and some are still nomadic.

The Tibetans live in the high mountainous Qinghai-Tibetan plateau, the traditional home of Lama Buddhism. An animal commonly associated with Tibet is the yak, which is used as a draught animal, for transport in the highlands, and whose milk products form a staple of Tibetan diet.

The Zhuang are one of China's largest minority nationalities (altogether about 10 million people). They live in Guangxi in subtropical southern China. The Zhuang, like the Han, are principally an agricultural people.

What do you know about China?

1. The largest city in China is a) Shanghai, b) Beijing, c) Guangzhou.
2. The largest nationality in China is a) Mongolian, b) Zhuang, c) Han.
3. China's population is a) about 10 million, b) about 100 million, c) over 1000 million.
4. China's longest border is with a) Korea, b) Kazakhstan, c) Vietnam, d) Mongolia, e) Russia.
5. China is a) much larger than Australia, b) much smaller than Australia, c) about the same size as Australia.
6. Which animal is not found in China? a) tiger, b) panda, c) giraffe.

1.2 Hello!

你好！

你 好！
Nǐ hǎo!

彼得，你 好！
Bǐdé, nǐ hǎo!

老师，您 好！
Lǎoshī, nín hǎo!

妈妈，您 好！
Māma, nín hǎo!

你们 好！
Nǐmen hǎo!

同学们，
Tóngxuémen,

你们 好！
nǐmen hǎo!

"你好！"

There are many ways of saying 'hello' in Chinese. People often greet each other by asking questions such as 'Where are you going?', 'Have you eaten?', or, on someone's arrival, saying 'You're here!'

Foreign names in Chinese

Foreign names are usually transliterated into Chinese. That is, they are written in Chinese characters which sound similar to the original pronunciation, e.g.

Bǐdé (彼得) Peter
Mǎlì (玛丽) Mary
Ālún Shǐmìsī
(阿伦·史密斯)
Alan Smith

再见！

Zàijiàn!

老师，再见！
Lǎoshī, zàijiàn!

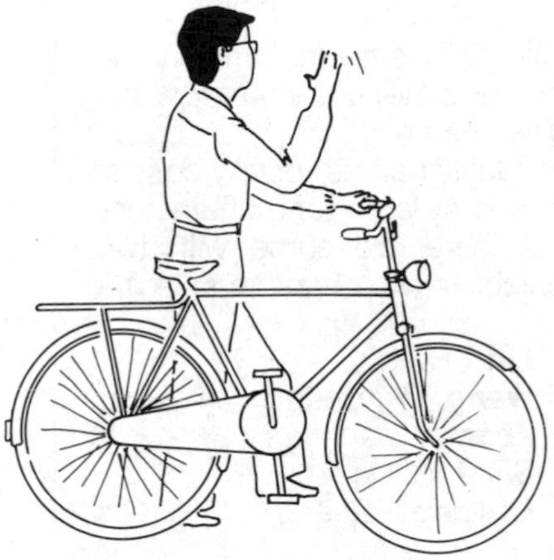

爸爸，再见！
Bàba, zàijiàn!

Notes:

1. *Men* (们) is a suffix that is placed after a pronoun or a noun which denotes a person, e.g.

nǐ	you (singular)	*nǐmen*	you (plural)
tóngxué	schoolmate	*tóngxuémen*	schoolmates
lǎoshī	teacher	*lǎoshīmen*	teachers

2. *Lǎoshī, nín hǎo*! – *Nǐ* (你) and *nín* (您) both mean 'you' (singular). *Nín* is the polite form of *nǐ*. You should use *nín* when you are addressing adults (e.g. elderly people, teachers, parents) or people you do not know well.

Nǐ tīngdǒng le ma? →
Greet them! →

LEARN TO READ page 21

LEARN TO WRITE Lesson 1 page 28

你听懂了吗？

(Nǐ tīngdǒng le ma?)

1. Which is true?
   a) Only Anna and the boy are in the room.
   b) There is somebody else in the room.
   c) Anna only saw the boy in the room.
2. This is a dialogue between:
   a) The boy and his schoolmates.
   b) The boy and the teacher.
   c) The students and the teacher.
3. Which is more probable?
   a) Anna is greeting her schoolmate.
   b) Anna is greeting the headmaster.
   c) Anna is greeting her big brother.
4. Which is most probable?
   a) Mary is going out.
   b) Mary has just arrived home.
   c) Mary is at David's home.

Greet them!

Perhaps you would also like to greet some other members of your family? For example, your

elder sister	jiějie
younger sister	mèimei
elder brother	gēge
younger brother	dìdi

1.3 How are you?

From now on, pinyin will be dropped from beneath all the characters you have learned in the Learn to Read and Learn to Write sections. In the following texts, a small circle (∘) under a character will indicate that its pinyin reading has been left out because it is a character whose pronunciation you know. If a line consists entirely of characters you know, both pinyin and symbols will be dropped.

Chinese names

Chinese (Han) names are made up of:

FAMILY NAME + GIVEN NAME

In Chinese, the family name (or surname) comes *before* the given name.

Family names usually consist of one syllable (one character), but there are some with two syllables (two characters), e.g.

Lín *Fāng*
Wáng *Yúnzhēn*
Zhāng *Jiànhuá*
Sīmǎ *Qīng*
Ōuyáng *Chéng*

Note that the given names are made up of one or two syllables. Most Chinese names are like this. A person's title is placed *after* the name, e.g.

Lǐ ***lǎoshī*** or
Lǐ Guóhuá ***lǎoshī***

你好吗？ (Nǐ hǎo ma?)

1. A: 你 好 吗？
∘ ∘ ma?

B: 挺 好 的，您 呢？
Tǐng ∘ de, nín ne?

A: 也 挺 好 的。
Yě tǐng ∘ de.

2. 彼得： 喂，林 方！
Bǐdé: Wèi, Lín Fāng!

林 方： 彼得！
Lín Fāng: Bǐdé!

彼得： 你 好 吗？
Bǐdé: Nǐ ∘ ma?

林 方： 挺 好 的。你 呢？
Lín Fāng: Tǐng ∘ de. ∘ ne?

彼得： 还 可以。
Bǐdé: Hái kěyǐ.

Notes:

1. When two or more 3rd tone syllables follow each other, only the last one is pronounced in the 3rd tone, the preceding ones are pronounced as 2nd tones, e.g.

   Nǐ hǎo! is pronounced as *Ní hǎo*!

2. *Ne* (呢) is used to make a 'tag' question, e.g.

   *Wǒ hěn hǎo, **nǐ ne?*** I'm fine, how about you?

   Of course, the listener must know what you are referring to in order to make sense of the question.

3. *Tǐng hǎo de* (挺好的) is a phrase meaning 'quite well (good)'.

4. Note that the subject *wǒ* (我) is omitted in the sentences

   (Wǒ) Tǐng hǎo de, nǐ ne?
   (Wǒ) Yě tǐng hǎo de.
   (Wǒ) Hái kěyǐ, nǐ ne?
   (Wǒ) Tǐng hǎo de.

   You may do this if you are sure you will not be misunderstood.

5. *Wèi, Lín Fāng! – Wèi* (喂) is an exclamation used to attract someone's attention.

Find the Chinese →
Nǐ tīngdǒng le ma? →

Find the Chinese

I'm fine, too.
I'm all right.
…, how about you?
I'm fine.
How are you?

你听懂了吗？

(Nǐ tīngdǒng le ma?)

1. Which is more probable?
   a) The girl prefers not to talk to Peter at the moment.
   b) The girl is feeling rather unhappy about something.
2. Which is correct?
   a) The girl's given name is Wang.
   b) Her surname is Liping.
   c) Her surname is Wang and her given name is Liping.

说汉语一 (Shuō Hànyǔ Yī)

1. 玛丽： 彼得！
   Mǎlì: Bǐdé!

   请 进，请 进！
   Qǐng jìn, qǐng jìn!

   彼得： 你 好 吗？
   Bǐdé: ◦ ◦ ma?

   玛丽： 挺 好 的，你 呢？
   Mǎlì: Tǐng ◦ de, ◦ ne?

   彼得： 还 可以
   Bǐdé: Hái kěyǐ.

玛丽： 请 坐。
Mǎlì: Qǐng zuò.

彼得： 谢谢。
Bǐdé: Xièxie.

2. 林 方： 你 好 吗？
Lín Fāng: 。 。 ma?

张 建华： 还 可以。
Zhāng Jiànhuá: Hái kěyǐ.

你 怎么样？ 好 吗？
。 zěnmeyàng ? 。 。?

林 方： 挺 好 的。
Lín Fāng: Tǐng 。 de.

坐 吧。
Zuò ba.

Note:
Ba (吧) at the end of a sentence softens the tone of the sentence and indicates a suggestion or request.

Find the Chinese →
该你了！**(Gāi nǐ le!)** →

LEARN TO READ page 22

Find the Chinese

Thank you.
Please come in.
Do sit down.
How are things with you?
Mary.

该你了！ (Gāi nǐ le!)

Act out a scene where a friend calls on you and you invite him or her in.

How to pronounce it?

Modern Standard Chinese (or *putonghua*) has 404 basic **syllables**. Some of these syllables are made up of simply a vowel sound, e.g.

i *ai* *iou*

Most syllables however, are made up of two components, which are called the **initial** and the **final**, e.g.

Syllable	=	initial	+	final
ma		m		*a*
tai		t		*ai*
pang		p		*ang*

When uttering a syllable in Chinese, apart from pronouncing the initial and final in the right way, you must use the correct **tone** (i.e. the correct pitch). Chinese is thus a tonal language.

There are four basic tones in Chinese. These are called the **1st tone**, **2nd tone**, **3rd tone** and **4th tone**, and are indicated by the use of marks placed above the (main) vowel in the final of the syllable, e.g.

1st tone	2nd tone	3rd tone	4th tone
mā	má	mǎ	mà

The 1st tone may be described as a rather long high pitch, the 2nd tone as a long rising pitch, the 3rd tone a low dipping and then rising pitch, and the 4th tone a rather abrupt falling pitch. On a scale of 5, the four tones would look like this:

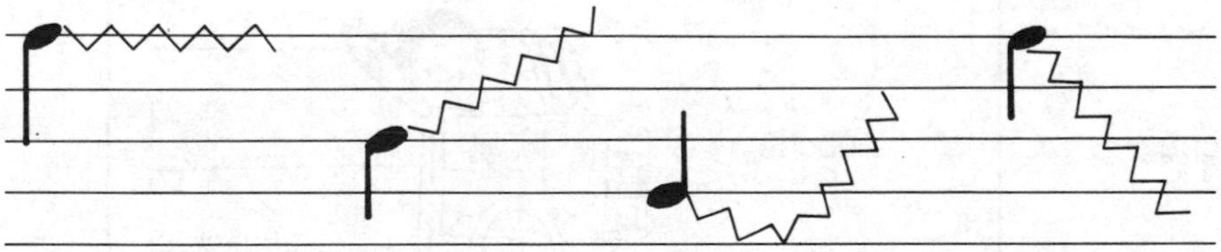

1st tone 2nd tone 3rd tone 4th tone

Apart from these four basic tones, there is a **neutral tone**, which has no set pitch. The actual pitch of a syllable pronounced in the neutral tone depends on the tone preceding it. Generally syllables which are unstressed in a sentence are pronounced in the netural tone. The netural tone is indicated by a small circle above the vowel or no tone mark at all, e.g.

må or ma

Tones are important!

Just as you have to sing each note in a song at its correct pitch for other people to know what song it is, you have to pronounce Chinese words with the correct tones for people to understand what you are saying. Also, when you are uttering a syllable, a change in tone could change its meaning! Take the syllable *ma* for instance.

1st tone	2nd tone	3rd tone	4th tone
mā	má	mǎ	mà
mother	to feel numb	horse	to scold

It is obvious that you will have to be careful when saying, for example, *Where's Mum? or Mum's coming*! or when mentioning these activities or things:

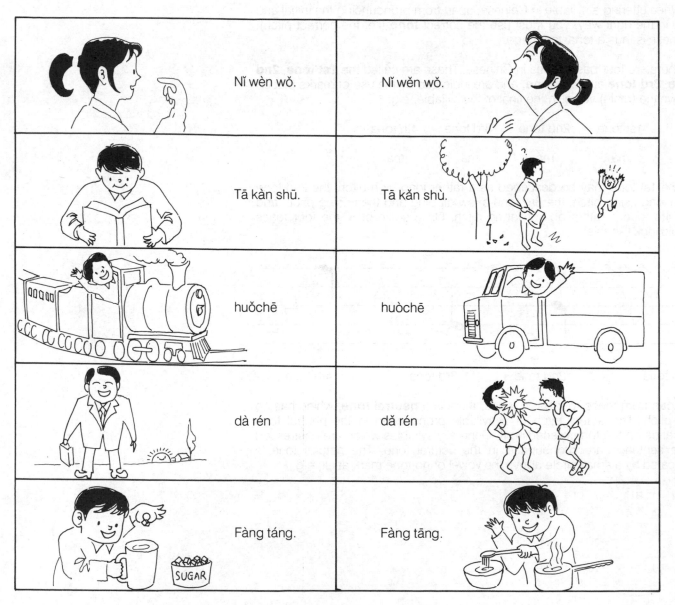

	Nǐ wèn wǒ.	Nǐ wěn wǒ.	
	Tā kàn shū.	Tā kǎn shù.	
	huǒchē	huòchē	
	dà rén	dǎ rén	
	Fàng táng.	Fàng tāng.	

1.4 What is your name?

请问，你叫什么名字？

(Qǐngwèn, nǐ jiào shénme míngzi?)

你们 好！

我 叫 林 方。

Wǒ jiào 。 。

我 叫 李 国华。

Wǒ jiào Lǐ Guóhuá.

我 叫 张 建华。

Wǒ jiào Zhāng Jiànhuá.

他 叫 什么 名字？

Tā jiào shénme míngzi?

他 叫 张 建华。

Tā jiào Zhāng Jiànhuá.

她 叫 什么 名字？

Tā jiào shénme míngzi?

她 叫 安娜。

Tā jiào Ānnà.

> **我叫什么名字？**
>
> See page 173 for a list of English names with their Chinese pronunciations.

他 姓 什么？
Tā xìng shénme?

他 姓 张。
Tā xìng Zhāng.

林

她 呢？
Tā ne?

她 姓 林。
Tā xìng ◦

请问，你 叫 什么 名字？
Qǐngwèn, ◦ jiào shénme míngzi?

请问，你 姓 什么？
Qǐngwèn, ◦ xìng shénme?

Notes:

1. *Nǐ jiào shénme míngzi?* – When someone asks you your name in Chinese, that person might say:

   Nǐ jiào shénme míngzi? or just *Nǐ jiào shénme?*

   You may reply by giving:

   a) your full name (family name and given name), e.g.

      Wǒ jiào Líndá Shǐmìsī. (My name's Linda Smith.)

   b) or, in an informal situation, with just your given name, e.g.

      Wǒ jiào Líndá. (My name's Linda.)

   Chinese names, unlike English names, are usually expressed in full, even in an informal situation. That is why in the above situation Lin Fang gives her full name (family name plus given name) while Peter and Anna give only their given name. Lin Fang's fellow students will also call her Lin Fang in everyday situations without sounding stiff or formal.

   There are, of course, also ways of addressing people you know well which are more informal. You will learn some of these in later lessons.

2. *Nǐ xìng shénme?* – Chinese people will often ask someone what their family name or xìng (姓) is:

Nǐ ***xìng*** *shénme?* (What is your family name?)

or by the polite formula (which you should also learn to use, especially when you are addressing adults.):

Nín ***guì xìng?*** 您贵姓？

您 贵 姓？
Nín guì xìng?

Nǐ	jiào	shénme míngzi?
Wǒ	jiào	Zhāng Jiànhuá. Bǐdé

Nín	guì xìng?	
Wǒ	xìng	Zhāng. Shǐmìsī

Find the Chinese →
该你了！**(Gāi nǐ le!)** →

Find the Chinese

What is his name?
May I ask …?
Her family name is Lin.
My name is Lin Fang.

该你了！ (Gāi nǐ le!)

Choose a name (e.g. someone famous) which you will pretend for the next few minutes is your own name. Divide into small groups and ask each other your names. After a few minutes, one person in each group can tell the class what the (adopted) name of each member of the group is. You can pronounce the adopted names in an English way but the rest of the question and answer must be in Chinese.

我是学生 (Wǒ shì xuésheng)

1. 你 好！

我 叫 彼得。
Wǒ jiào Bǐdé.

我 是 学生。
Wǒ shì xuésheng.

2. 同学们 好！

Tóngxuémen 。!

我 叫 李 国华。

Wǒ jiào Lǐ Guóhuá.

我 是 老师。

Wǒ shì 。 。

3. 我 叫 张 建华。

Wǒ jiào Zhāng Jiànhuá.

我 不 是 老师。

Wǒ bú shì 。 。

我 是 学生。

Wǒ shì xuésheng.

4. 我 是 林 方。

Wǒ shì 。 。

我 也 是 学生。

Wǒ 。 shì xuésheng.

Note:

Bú shì – Note that if you look in the wordlist, *bù* (不) is 4th tone, but in *bú shì* (不是), *bù* is 2nd tone. This is because *bù* changes its tone from a 4th tone to a 2nd tone when it appears before a 4th tone syllable.

bù → *bú* + 4th tone syllable
bú shì
bú jiào

Tā		shì xuésheng.
Tā	yě	shì xuésheng.
Tā	bú	shì xuésheng.
Wǒ	yě bú	shì xuésheng.

他 是 谁？
Tā shì shéi?

他 是 彼得。
Tā shì Bǐdé.

他 是 我 的 同学。
Tā shì wǒ ◦ tóngxué.

她 是 谁？
Tā shì shéi?

她 是 我 的 老师。
Tā shì wǒ

他们 是 谁？
Tāmen shì shéi?

他们 是 我 的 朋友。
Tāmen shì wǒ ◦ péngyou.

你 是 谁？
Nǐ shì shéi?

我 是 你 的 汉语 老师！
Wǒ shì ◦ ◦ Hànyǔ ◦ ◦!

Note:
Wǒ de péngyou – *'Wǒ de …'* (我的…) means 'my …'. How would you express 'your', 'his', 'their', 'Anna's'?

wǒ nǐ tā wǒmen nǐmen tāmen Ānnà	de	péngyou tóngxué lǎoshī

How would you say 'their friend', 'Anna's classmate', 'our teacher'?

他（她）是谁？

Tā (tā) shì shéi?

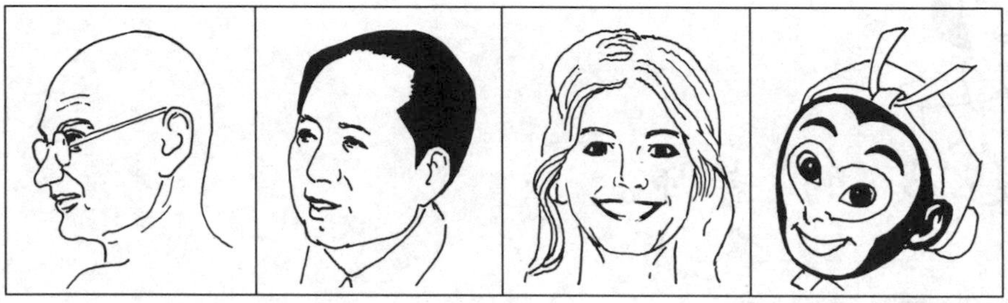

他们是谁？

Tāmen shì shéi?

Find the Chinese →
Nǐ tīngdǒng le ma? →

LEARN TO READ page 22

LEARN TO WRITE Lesson 2 page 35

Find the Chinese

Who are they?
I'm a student too.
He's my classmate.
Who's she?
I'm not a teacher.
She's my teacher.

你听懂了吗？

(Nǐ tīngdǒng le ma?)

1. Which of these statements are true?
   a) The teacher's surname is Lin.
   b) The teacher's surname is Chen.
   c) The teacher teaches Chinese.
2. Which of these statements is true?
   a) i) The boy and the girl are on the school playground
      ii) They are on a bus.
      iii) They are in the school office.
   b) i) The girl came to see her teacher.
      ii) She came to see a fellow student.
      iii) The boy is not known to the girl.

1.5 What country are you from?

我是中国人 (Wǒ shì Zhōngguórén)

1. 我 是 张 建华。
   ○ ○ Zhāng Jiànhuá.

   我 是 中国人。
   ○ shi○ Zhōngguórén.

   我 是 安娜。
   ○ ○ Ānnà.

   我 是 澳大利亚人。
   ○ ○ Àodàlìyàrén.

2. A: 张 建华 是 中国人 吗？
   Zhāng Jiànhuá ○ Zhōngguórén ○?

   B: 是，他 是 中国人。
   ○ ○ ○ Zhōngguórén.

   A: 安娜 也 是 中国人 吗？
   Ānnà ○ ○ Zhōngguórén ○?

   B: 不，她 是 澳大利亚人。
   ○, ○ ○ Àodàlìyàrén.

Foreign place names

Foreign place names are also usually expressed in Chinese by transliteration, using Chinese characters which approximate the original pronunciation of the place name, e.g.

Àodàlìyà (Australia)
Xīní (Sydney)
Ādéláidé (Adelaide)

Notes:
Nǐ shì Àodàlìyàrén ma? – Adding *ma* (吗) to the end of a statement turns it into a question. More examples:

Tā shì Lǐ lǎoshī.	*Tā shì Lǐ lǎoshī ma?*
Tā shì Zhōngguórén.	*Tā shì Zhōngguórén ma?*

And here is how you might answer such questions:

	Tā shì	Àodàlìyàrén	ma?
Shì, Bù,	tā shì tā bú shì	Àodàlìyàrén. Àodàlìyàrén.	

As you can see, answering *Shì …* or *Bù …* is somewhat like saying 'Yes, …' or 'No, …' in English.

Find the Chinese →
该你了！**(Gāi nǐ le!)** →

哪国人？ (Něi guó rén?)

A: 请问，你 是 哪 国 人？
Qǐngwèn, nǐ ◦ něi guó rén?

B: 我 是 澳大利亚人。
◦ ◦ Àodàlìyàrén.

A: 您 呢？您 是 哪 国 人？
Ní n ◦? Nín ◦ něi guó rén?

C: 我 是 日本人。
◦ ◦ Rìběnrén.

Find the Chinese

No, she's Australian.
Is Zhang Jianhua Chinese?
I'm Chinese.

该你了！ (Gāi nǐ le!)

Tā shì Ānnà ma?
Tā jiào Bǐdé ma?
Nǐmen de lǎoshī xìng Lǐ ma?
Bǐdé shì xuésheng ma?
Nǐ hǎo ma?
Nǐ xué Hànyǔ ma?

What is the questioner trying to find out? How might you answer the questions?

A: 你们 学 汉语 吗？
Nǐmen ∘ Hànyǔ ma?

B: 我 学 汉语。
∘ xue Hànyǔ

C: 我 也 学 汉语。
∘ ∘ ∘ Hànyǔ

Note:
Ānnà shì něi guó rén? – Něi guó rén? （哪国人？） literally means 'person from which country'.

Nǐ Bǐdé	shì	něi guó rén?
Wǒ Tā	shì	Àodàlìyàrén.

说汉语二 (Shuō Hànyǔ Èr)

A: 你们 是 中国人 吗？
∘ ∘ ∘ Zhōngguórén ∘?

B: 不，我们 是 日本人。
Bù, ∘ ∘ ∘ Rìběnrén.

A: 哦，对不起。
Ò, duìbuqǐ.

B: 没 关系。
Méi guānxi.

A: 你们 也 学 汉语 吗?
。 。 。 。 Hànyǔ 。?

B: 是，我们 也 学 汉语。
。, 。 。 。 。 Hànyǔ.

Find the Chinese →
该你了！(Gāi nǐ le!) →
Nǐ tīngdǒng le ma? →

LEARN TO READ page 23

LEARN TO WRITE Lesson 3 page 36

哪国?

Below is a list of foreign countries. Can you tell from the pronunciation what the English names of the countries listed are? (You will need some help from your teacher!) If you want to express the word for a national of any country, just add *rén* (人) to the name of the country.

Xīnxīlán 新西兰
Jiā'nádà 加拿大
Yuènán 越南
Mǎláixīyà 马来西亚
Xīnjiāpō 新加坡
Yìndùníxīyà 印度尼西亚
Jiǎnpǔzhài 柬埔寨
Yìndù 印度
Yìdàlì 意大利
Éluósī 俄罗斯
Xīlà 希腊
Xībānyá 西班牙
Líbānèn 黎巴嫩
Hánguó 韩国
Jīnbābùwéi 津巴布韦
Mòxīgē 墨西哥
Bābùyà Xīnjǐnèiyà 巴布亚新几内亚
Tǔ'ěrqí 土耳其
Tàiguó 泰国
Sīlǐlánkǎ 斯里兰卡
Bōlán 波兰
Luómǎníyà 罗马尼亚
Fēilǜbīn 菲律宾
Hélán 荷兰
Xiōngyálì 匈牙利
Yīngguó 英国
Měiguó 美国
Rìběn 日本
Fǎguó 法国
Déguó 德国

Find the Chinese

Oh, I'm sorry.
That's all right.
Yes, we study Chinese too.
No, we're Japanese.
What country are you from?

该你了！ (Gāi nǐ le!)

Imagine that you and your friend(s) meet a Chinese student in the school playground and you have a conversation with him or her What would you say? Act the dialogue out with some of your classmates.

你听懂了吗?

(Nǐ tīngdǒng le ma?)

1. a) The man and woman are Japanese tourists.
   b) They are Chinese.
   c) They are Australians.
2. a) Both Mr Fang and Mrs Fang understand some Japanese.
   b) Mrs Fang does not understand any Japanese, but Mr Fang does.
3. a) Robin and Frank are both learning Chinese at school.
   b) Neither of them is learning Chinese at school.
   c) Robin is learning Chinese at school.

学会认字 (Xuéhuì rèn zì)

1.2

Before reading the text, listen to the recording and answer the questions.

1. The conversation was between
   a) teachers
   b) students
   c) teacher and students

2. There was
   a) only one student present
   b) more than one student present
   c) no student present

汉字表 (Hànzì biǎo)

			As in
老	lǎo	*(as in* lǎoshī)	老师
师	shī	*teacher*	
你	nǐ	*you*	你好！
好	hǎo	*good; well*	
们	men	*(pluralising suffix)*	你们
再	zài	*again*	再见！
见	jiàn	*see*	

Text

A: 老师，你好！

B: 你们好！

(later)

A: 再见！

B: 再见！

C: 再见！

1.3

Before reading the text, listen to the recording and answer the questions.

True or false?
1. The girl's name is Lin Fang.
2. The girl wanted to know how the boy was.

汉字表 (Hànzì biǎo)

			As in
林	lín	*(surname); forest*	林方
方	fāng	*(name); square*	
吗	ma	*(question particle)*	你好吗?
挺	tǐng	*rather, quite*	挺好的
的	de	*(structural particle)*	
呢	ne	*(sentence particle)*	你呢?
也	yě	*also*	也挺好的

Text

G: 林方!你好吗?
B: 挺好的,你呢?
G: 也挺好的。

1.4

Before reading the text, listen to the recording and answer the questions.

True or false?
1. The boy does not know Lin Fang.
2. The boy is not a student.
3. Lin Fang is a teacher.
4. Both Lin Fang and the boy are students.

汉字表 (Hànzì biǎo)

			As in
叫	jiào	*to be called*	你叫什么?

什	shén	*(as in* shénme)	什么
么	me	*(as in* shénme)	
名	míng	*name*	名字
字	zì	*character, word*	
我	wǒ	*I; me*	我们
是	shì	*am, is; are*	
学	xué	*to learn*	学生
生	shēng	*(as in* xuésheng)	

Text

B: 你叫什么名字？
G: 我叫林方。

B: 你也是学生吗？
G: 是，我也是学生。

1.5

Before reading the text, listen to the recording and answer the questions.

True or false?
1. The man thought that the students were teachers.
2. The woman is an Australian teacher.
3. The woman is a Chinese student.
4. The teachers are Chinese.
5. Both teachers are language teachers.

汉字表 (Hànzì biǎo)

			As in
他	tā	*he, him*	他们
中	zhōng	*middle*	中国

国	guó	*country*	
人	rén	*person*	中国人
她	tā	*she, her*	她们
不	bù	*not*	不是
澳	ào	(*as in* Àodàlìyà)	澳大利亚
大	dà	*big*	
利	lì	(*as in* Àodàlìyà)	
亚	yà	(*as in* Àodàlìyà)	
汉	hàn	Han; Chinese	汉语
语	yǔ	language	

Text

M: 你们是澳大利亚人吗?
W: 我们是澳大利亚人。

M: 你们是老师吗?
W: 不，我们不是老师。
我们是学生。
我们学汉语。

(pointing to two persons nearby)

他们是中国人。
他们是我们的汉语老师。

动动脑筋!

(Dòngdong nǎojīn!)

This is a phrase literally meaning 'get your brain moving' or 'use your brain'. See if you can *dòngdòng nǎojīn* and guess what these words might mean. They are made up of characters you know.

老人
好人
国语

Summary

1.2 Hello!

Now you can:

greet someone and say goodbye:

Nǐ hǎo! 你好！
Māma, nín hǎo! 妈妈，您好！
Lǎoshī, zàijiàn! 老师，再见！
Zàijiàn! 再见！

Grammar and usage reference

Foreign names in Chinese page 4
Men (们) pluralising suffix page 5
Nǐ (你) and *nín* (您) page 5

1.3 How are you?

Now you can:

ask someone 'How are you?':

Nǐ hǎo ma? 你好吗？
Nǐ zěnmeyàng, hǎo ma? 你怎么样，好吗？

possible replies:

Tǐng hǎo de. 挺好的。
Hái kěyǐ. 还可以。
Tǐng hǎo de, nǐ ne? 挺好的，你呢？

invite someone in:

Qǐng jìn! 请进！

invite someone to sit down:

Qǐng zuò. 请坐。
Zuò ba. 坐吧。

say 'thank you':

Xièxie. 谢谢。

Useful expressions
Tǐng hǎo de（挺好的）*Quite well (good).*
Hái kěyǐ（还可以）*All right. So so.*

Grammar and usage reference
Chinese names page 6
Tone change when two 3rd tone syllables follow each other page 7
Ne（呢）used to make a 'tag' question page 7
Wǒ（我）as subject sometimes omitted if understood page 7
Wèi!（喂!）exclamation to attract attention page 7
Ba（吧）used to soften tone of sentence page 8

1.4 What is your name?

Now you can:

ask what someone's name is:
(Qǐngwèn), nǐ jiào shénme míngzi?（请问），你叫什么名字?
Tā jiào shénme míngzi? 她叫什么名字?
(Qǐngwèn), nǐ xìng shénme?（请问），你姓什么?

possible replies:
Wǒ jiào Ānnà. 我叫安娜。
Tā jiào Zhāng Jiànhuá. 他叫张建华。
Wǒ xìng Lín. 我姓林。

identify yourself or others:
Wǒ shì Lín Fāng. 我是林方。
Wǒ shì xuésheng. 我是学生。
Wǒ bú shì lǎoshī. 我不是老师。
Tā shì Lǐ Guóhuá. 他是李国华。
Tā shì wǒmen de lǎoshī. 他是我们的老师。

ask who someone is:
Tā shì shéi? 他是谁?

Useful expressions
Nín guì xìng?（您贵姓?）(*polite way of asking someone's surname*)
Qǐngwèn,...（请问，...）*Please may I ask ...*

Grammar and usage reference
Asking someone's name page 12
Xìng（姓）used to ask about family names page 13
Bù（不）pronounced in second tone page 14
De（的）used to indicate possession page 15

1.5 What country are you from?

Now you can:

ask about nationality:
Nín shì něi guó rén? 您是哪国人？
Nǐmen shì Zhōngguórén ma? 你们是中国人吗？

possible replies:
Wǒ shì Àodàlìyàrén. 我是澳大利亚人。
Bù, wǒmen shì Rìběnrén. 不，我们是日本人。

apologise:
Duìbuqǐ. 对不起。

respond to someone's apology:
Méi guānxi. 没关系。

ask if someone is learning Chinese:
Nǐmen xué Hànyǔ ma? 你们学汉语吗？

possible replies:
Shì, wǒmen xué Hànyǔ. 是，我们学汉语。
Bù, wǒmen bù xué Hànyǔ. 不，我们不学汉语。

Useful expressions
Duìbuqǐ（对不起）*I'm sorry.*
Méi guānxi（没关系）*Never mind.*

Grammar and usage reference
Foreign place names page 17
Ma（吗）turns a statement into a question page 18
Shì, ...（是，......）*Bù,...*（不，......）compared with 'Yes, ...' and 'No, ...' page 18
Něi guó rén?（哪国人）page 19

Vocabulary reference
Place names (countries) page 20

学会写字 第一课 (Xuéhuì xiě zì Dì-yī kè)

I. Chinese characters – how they evolved

c.6000	SHANG 1600–1100 BC	ZHOU 1100–221 BC	WARRING STATES 475–221 BC	QIN 221–207 BC

Chinese characters are believed to have originated some 6000 years ago.

These marks found on pottery of the neolithic age are the beginnings of a pictographic script.

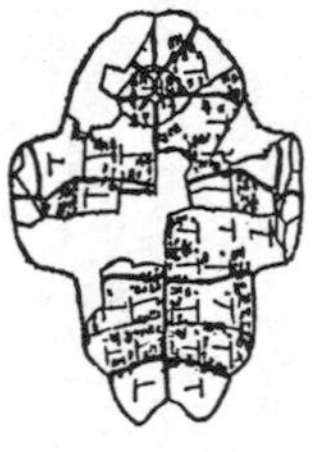

These writings on bones and tortoise shells date back to the Shang period. Known as *jiágǔwén*, it is the earliest example of pictographic script found in China.

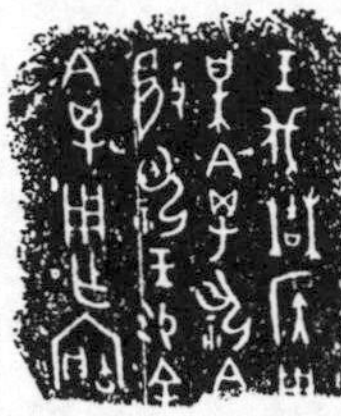

During the Zhou Dynasty, people used a simplified and modified form of *jiágǔwén*.

Characters or script were inscribed onto bronze vessels or written on bamboo slips which were tied together into "books".

Several states emerged during the Zhou Dynasty. They fought each other and so this period became known as the Warring States period.

There was a lot of variation in the way characters were written in these states. Sometimes the same character had different meanings.

In 221 BC the State of Qin unified China and the Qin dynasty was founded.

A series of important reforms were begun by the First Emperor (known as Qin Shi Huang).

It was decreed that the whole country should have the same writing system.

A system with characters based mainly on those of the State of Qin was adopted as standard, and stone tablets with characters carved on them were set up as examples of the new script.

Towards the end of emperor Qin Shih Huang's reign the writing brush was in general use. It was difficult to write rounded strokes with the soft tip of a brush and so a new character form known as *lishū* came into being.

Lìshū marked the beginning of the development of the Chinese characters we see today.

Here are some examples of how the early pictographic script evolved into characters.

RÌ (sun)	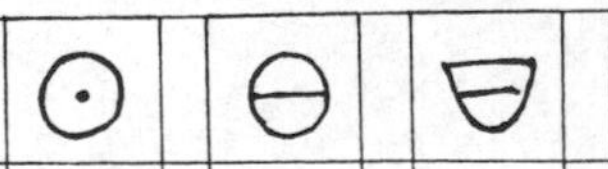	日	日
YUÈ (moon)	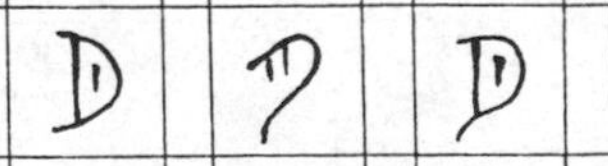	月	月
SHUǏ (water)	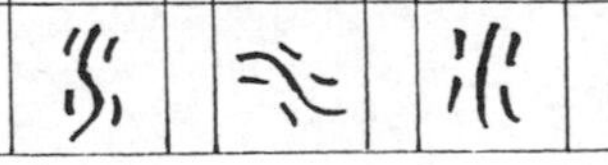	水	水

HAN 206 BC–23 AD	**THREE KINGDOMS** 220–280 AD	**EASTERN JIN** 265–316 AD

During the Han dynasty and the period of the Three Kingdoms different styles of character writing evolved.

By the Eastern Jin dynasty there were three main styles of characters in use. These can be seen even to this day.

Kǎishū, or regular script, has clearly written strokes. It is most often seen in printing, in formal letters or documents, on signs etc. It is also the preferred style for students learning to write characters.

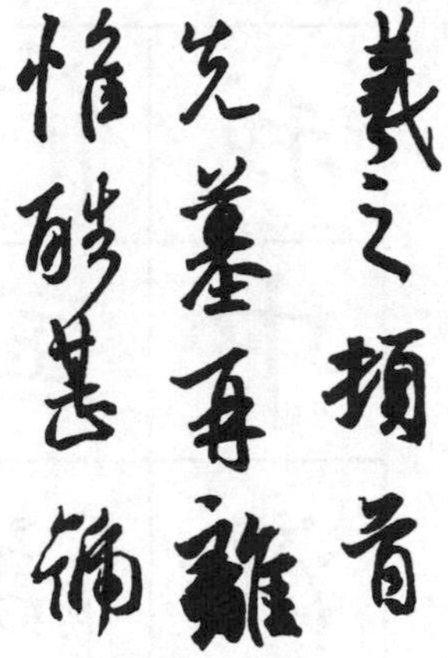

Xíngshū, or running script, is the style most often seen and used. It is not as formal as *kǎishū* but is easier to recognise than *cǎoshū*.

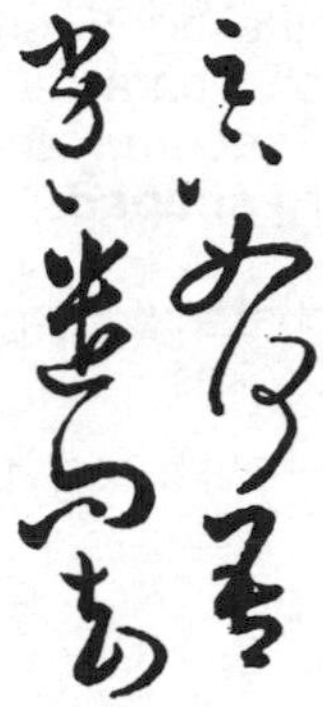

Cǎoshū, or cursive script, is written swiftly with strokes which flow together. It is difficult to learn and to read. Not many people use it.

Today one can still see the ancient forms of calligraphy as an art form used on inscriptions on painting, scrolls, decorative titles in books and magazines, seals and signs.

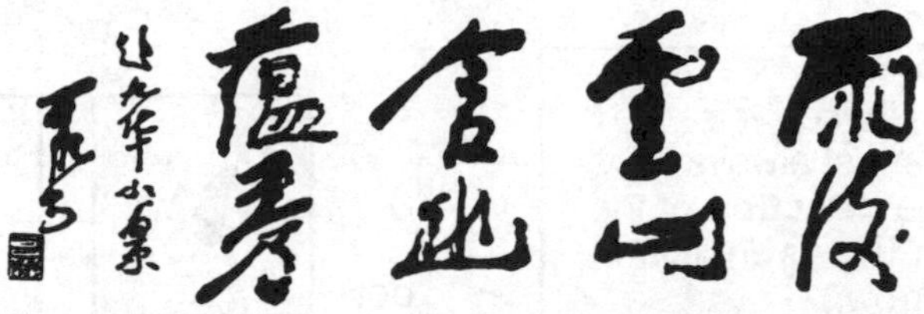

scroll

— calligraphy by Lǐ Kěrǎn

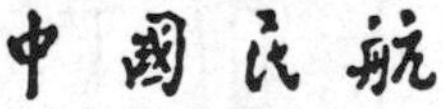

sign

seals

II. Writing Chinese characters

1. The basic strokes

If you look closely at the characters on the right you will notice that each character falls neatly into a square, and is therefore **square shaped**.

Also, each character is made up of lines, or strokes.

我	们	是
中	国	人
汉	语	课

A **stroke** is a single unbroken line drawn from the time you set your pen to paper and move it till the time you lift it off the paper.

There are some 30 basic strokes that go to make up all the characters in Chinese. We shall begin by learning how to write some of these basic strokes. Before you begin to use your practice sheets, read the rule in the box and take a close look at each basic stroke to see how they are written.

When writing these strokes, you must always:

a) follow the **direction** of the stroke. (This is indicated by the arrow.)

b) apply pressure as indicated by the different shades of black. (The darker it is the more the pressure applied.)

or

dot

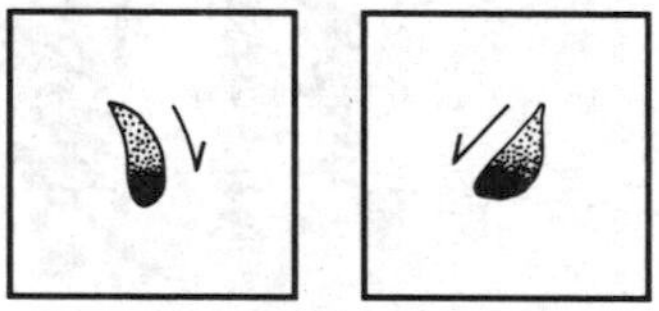

vertical

left-falling

hooked horizontal

hooked vertical

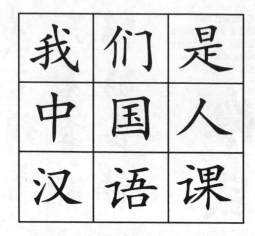

2. The character *nǐ*

This is the Chinese character for *nǐ*, meaning 'you'.

Let's write this character. You will be using all the basic strokes you have just learnt.

Before we begin, let's take a close look at the character *nǐ*.

Notice that *nǐ* is made up of two main **components** – one on the left and one on the right.

Also, the right component can be broken down into two smaller components, making three components 'A', 'B' and 'C'.

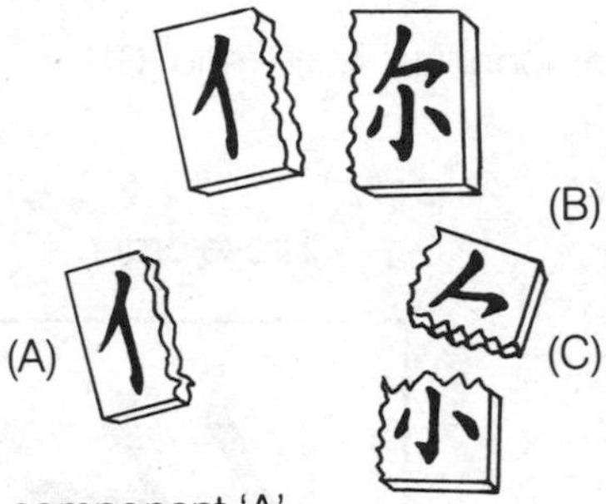

Step 1 Let's start by writing the component 'A'.

Start off with a left-falling stroke ...

... followed by a vertical stroke

Remember that you must always follow the direction of the stroke.

Also, note the position of the stroke in the square.

Step 2 We will now write the component 'B'.

Begin by writing a left-falling stroke

... followed by a hooked-horizontal.

Step 3 Now for the component 'C'.

A hooked-vertical …

… followed by two dots – first left, then right.

Step 4 Let us now put the components 'A', 'B' and 'C' together.

> When you write a character that has two or more strokes, you must follow a set sequence (indicated by the numbers at the beginning of each stroke as shown). This is called the **stroke-order**.

Stroke order:

How many strokes are there in the character *nǐ*?

3. The character *hǎo*

The character *hǎo* means 'good' or 'well'.

How many components does *hǎo* have?

To write *hǎo* we will need these basic strokes:

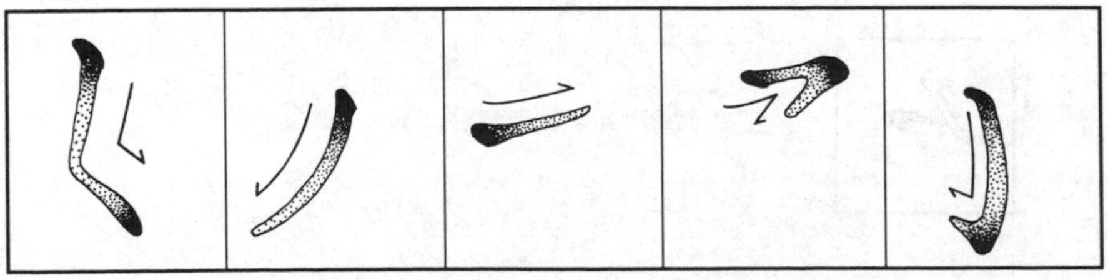

Step 1 The left component.

Step 2 The right component.

Notice that the hooked-vertical stroke is slightly bent.

Step 3 Let's put the left and right components together.

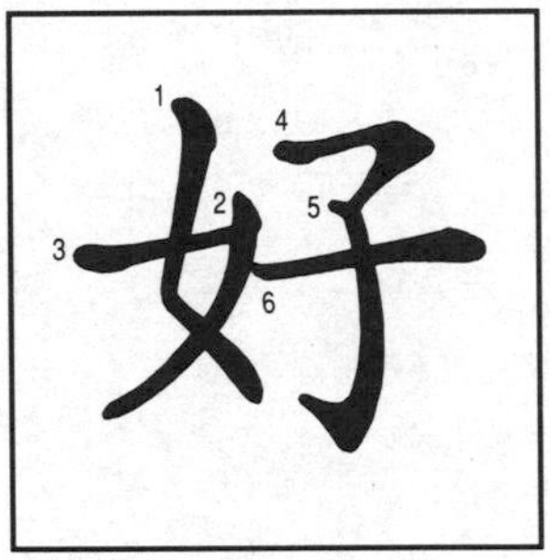

How many strokes are there in the character *hǎo*?

4. Some more characters to learn to write

Go through each character and see if you can identify its component parts.

MEN (a suffix) New basic stroke:

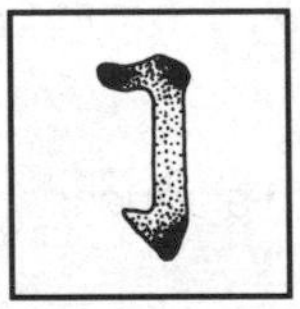

LǍO old New basic stroke:

SHĪ teacher; master

5. Sequence

When writing a character with more than one component, which component is written first?

Characters with a left and a right component:

e.g. 们 First left, then right.

Characters with a top and a bottom component:

e.g. 是 First top, then bottom.

6. Text

After practising with each character, try writing out these dialogues:

a) A: 老师，你好！

B: 你好！

b) A: 老师，你好！

B: 你们好！

学会写字 第二课 (Xuéhuì xiě zì Dì-èr kè)

汉字表 (Hànzì biǎo)

Basic stroke								
As in	我	我	叫	叫	是			

我	wǒ *I; me*	叫	jiào *to call; be called*
是	shì *am, are is*	学	xué *to study*
生	shēng *to be born*		

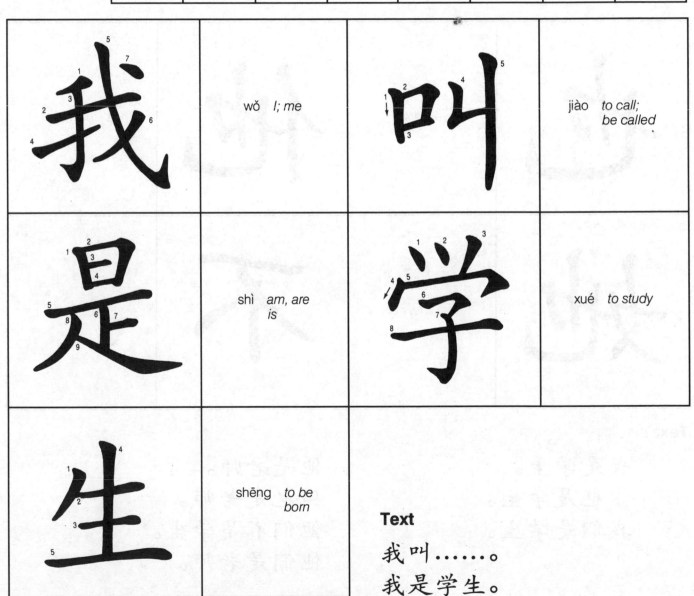

Text

我叫……。

我是学生。

学会写字 第三课 (Xuéhuì xiě zì Dì-sān kè)

汉字表 (Hànzì biǎo)

Basic stroke	
As in	也

也	yě *also*	他	tā *he, him*
她	tā *she, her*	不	bù *not*

Text

1. 我是学生。
   你也是学生。
   我们是学生。

2. 他是老师。
   她也是老师。
   他们不是学生。
   他们是老师。

UNIT 2 Meet my family

第二单元
Dì-èr dānyuán

我的一家
Wǒ de yì jiā

In this unit you will learn how to talk about where you live, the members of your family, and your pets. You will also learn how to count and how to say how old you are.

2.1 Meet my family

我的一家 (Wǒ de yì jiā)

Meet the families of two students, Zhao Wen and Zhang Jianqiu. Zhao Wen's family live in the southern city of Guangzhou, and Zhang Jianqiu's family live in China's capital, Beijing.

(Can you find Beijing and Guangzhou on the map of China? Do you know another version of the names of these two cities?)

1. 你们 好！

我 是 赵 文。
° ° Zhào Wén.

我 住 广州。
° zhù Guǎngzhōu.

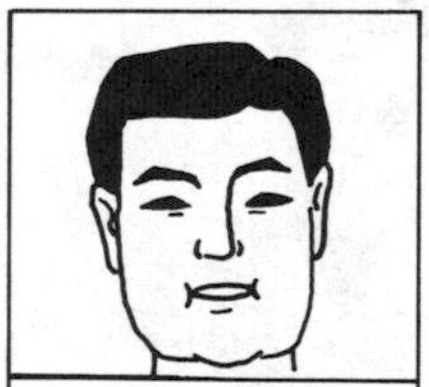

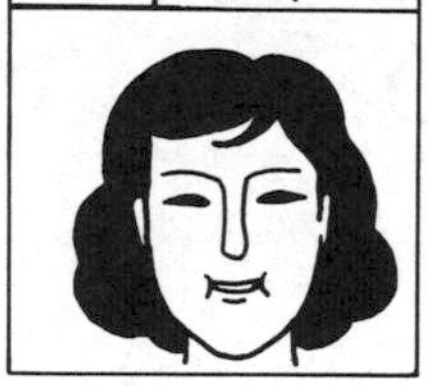

这 是 我 爸爸。
Zhè ° ° bàba.

这 是 我 妈妈。
Zhè ° ° māma.

这 是 我 姐姐 赵 云。
Zhè ° ° jiějie Zhào Yún.

她 是 大学生。
° ° dá ° shēng.

那 是 我 妹妹。
Nà ° ° mèimei.

她 叫 赵 青。她 上 小学。
° ° Zhào Qīng. ° shàng xiǎo°.

The family in China traditionally has been an extremely important social institution. One result of this is that there exists an enormous vocabulary of kinship terms which identify precisely the relationship between the members of a family.

An example of this is the terms you have just learned for 'brother' or 'sister' in Chinese which differ according to whether the brother or sister is older or younger than yourself. Many kinship terms are even more complicated. For example, you address an uncle by a different term depending on whether he is an uncle on your father's side or your mother's side. If he is an uncle by marriage, there is a whole new set of terms of address!

You may want to know the word for 'grandmother' and 'grandfather' so that you can describe your family. In Chinese, these terms differ according to which side of the family the grandparents belong to. Here they are:

your father's father
yéye (爷爷)
your father's mother
nǎinai (奶奶)
your mother's father
lǎoye (老爷)
your mother's mother
lǎolao (姥姥)

那 是 我 弟弟 赵 远。
Nà ∘ ∘ dìdi Zhào Yuǎn.

他 也 上 小学。
∘ ∘ shàng xiǎo ∘.

2. 你们 好!

我 是 张 建秋。
∘ ∘ Zhāng Jiànqiū.

我 住 北京。
∘ zhù Běijīng.

In China, parents choose a name for a child by selecting characters which express the parents' hopes for the child's future and also as an expression of the kind of qualities they hope will become part of his or her personality. For example, 勇 (*yǒng*), meaning 'courageous', for a boy's name or 美芳 (*Měifāng*) for a girl's name in which *měi* means 'beautiful' and *fāng* means 'fragrant'. 英 (*yīng*), meaning 'hero', 'heroine' or 'outstanding person', and 平 (*píng*), meaning 'peaceful', are often used in names for either girls or boys.

我 介绍 一下:
∘ jièshào yíxià:

这 是 我 爸爸。
Zhè ∘ ∘ bàba.

这 是 我 妈妈。
Zhè ∘ ∘ māma.

这 是 我 哥哥 建华。
Zhè ∘ ∘ gēge Jiànhuá.

他 上 中学。
∘ shàng ∘ ∘.

Note:
Note that you say '*wǒ bàba*' rather than '*wǒ de bàba*'. This is because when *wǒ*, *wǒmen*, *nǐ*, *nǐmen*, *tā*, *tāmen* are used with *de* (的) and refer to family members or relatives, the *de* is dropped. The boxes below show other examples.

Say:

Zhào Wén Lǐ lǎoshī péngyou bàba	de de de de	jiějie māma dìdi gēge

but:

wǒ nǐ tā wǒmen nǐmen tāmen	bàba māma gēge jiějie dìdi mèimei *(or other words indicating a family relationship)*

Now that you have met Zhao Wen's and Zhang Jianqiu's family, see if you can answer these questions:

请问，赵远的哥哥是谁?
Qǐngwèn, Zhào Yuǎn ◦ gēge ◦ shéi?

赵青的姐姐是谁?
Zhào Qīng ◦ jiějie ◦ shéi?

张建华的弟弟是谁?
Zhāng Jiànhuá ◦ dìdi ◦ shéi?

Zhè Nà	shì	wǒ	bàba. gēge dìdi jiějie mèimei

Find the Chinese →
该你了！**(Gāi nǐ le!)** →

Find the Chinese

This is my elder sister.
That's my younger sister.
I live in Beijing.
She goes to primary school.
That's my younger brother Zhao Yuan.
She's a university student.
I'll introduce you.

该你了！ (Gāi nǐ le!)

Now you can introduce your family to your class. If you do not have a family photo you can bring to class, draw a representative picture of your family (e.g. stick figures) which you can then introduce to your group. You can also now draw up your own family tree.

说汉语一 (Shuō Hànyǔ Yī)

珍妮： 你 好 吗？
Zhēnní:

大卫： 挺 好 的，你 呢？
Dàwèi:

珍妮： 还 可以。
Zhēnní: Hái kěyǐ.

大卫： 我 来 介绍 一下：
Dàwèi: ∘ lái jièshào yíxià.

这 是 珍妮。
Zhè ∘ Zhēnní.

这 是 我 的 朋友 花子。
Zhè ∘ ∘ ∘ péngyou Huāzǐ.

这 是 她 弟弟。
Zhè ∘ ∘ dìdi.

珍妮： 你们 好！
Zhēnní:

花子： 你 好！
Huāzǐ:

弟弟： 你 好！
Dìdi:

Find the Chinese →

In China it is customary to shake hands when introduced. What do people do in Australia when they are introduced? What about in other societies that you know of?

Japanese names in Chinese

Since the Japanese writing system also uses characters, Japanese names are read in Chinese simply by giving the characters their Chinese pronunciation instead of their Japanese one. Compare *Mǎdīng*, which is a transliteration of the English name 'Martin', with *Huāzǐ*, which is the Chinese pronunciation of the characters (花 子) for the Japanese name 'Hanako'.

Find the Chinese

I'm well, how about you?
I'm all right.
This is my friend Hanako.
Let me introduce you.
This is Martin.

他住哪儿？ (Tā zhù nǎr?)

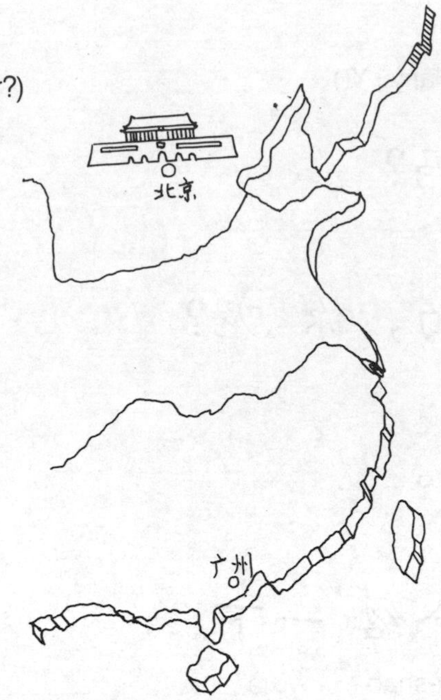

1. A: 赵 文 住 哪儿？
   Zhào Wén zhù nǎr?

   B: 赵 文 住 广州。
   Zhào Wén zhù Guǎngzhōu.

2. A: 张 建华 住 哪儿？
   Zhāng Jiànhuá zhù nǎr?

   B: 他 住 北京。
   ∘ zhù Běijīng.

请问，你 住 哪儿？
Qǐngwèn, ∘ zhù nǎr?

You can use this phrase to ask members of your class where he or she lives or where someone else lives. There is a list of Australian capital cities in the right-hand column, but if you want to say the name of your suburb or a town or city whose Chinese transliteration you do not know, just use the English pronunciation for the place name, e.g.

Wǒ zhù Ashgrove.

Nǐ Tā	**zhù**	**nǎr?**
Wǒ Tā	**zhù**	Běijīng. Guǎngzhōu Xīní Mò'ěrběn

你住哪儿？ →

LEARN TO READ page 60

LEARN TO WRITE Lesson 4 page 71

你住哪儿？

Where do you live? Where do your friends live? Here is a list of Australian capital cities for your reference.

Dá'ěrwén 达尔文
Bùlǐsībān 布里斯班
Xīní 悉尼
Kānpéilā 堪培拉
Mò'ěrběn 墨尔本
Huòbātè 霍巴特
Ādéláidé 阿德莱德
Pòsī 珀斯

2.2 My family

Counting 1 to 10

When you need to count to ten …

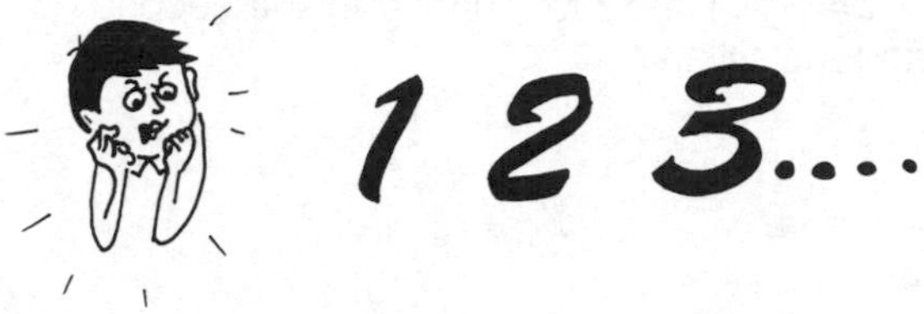

一 二 三 四 五 六 七 八 九 十

yī èr sān sì wǔ liù qī bā jiǔ shí

几 个 人?

Jǐ gè ◦?

一 个 学生

yí gè ◦ ◦

两 个 老师

liǎng gè ◦ ◦

三 个 朋友

sān gè péngyou

四 个 同学

sì gè tóng ◦

六 个 人

liù gè ◦

Notes:

1. *Gè* (个) belongs to the category of words called **measure words** which are placed between a number and a noun, e.g.

   *sì **gè** péngyou* (四个朋友)
   *liù **gè** rén* (六个人)

   In English, we sometimes use 'measure words', e.g. four loaves of bread, two cakes of soap. Can you think of any more?

2. Chinese nouns generally do not have a plural form. *Rén* (人) could mean 'a person' or 'people', *péngyou* (朋友) could mean 'friend' or 'friends' etc.

3. If you come across 'two' when counting or reading out numbers, it is read as *èr* (二), but when 'two' is followed by a measure word, i.e. when you are saying 'two of something', it is read as ***liǎng*** (两), e.g.

   liǎng gè rén.

4. The numbers *yī* (一) *qī* (七) *bā* (八) are pronounced in the second tone when followed by a fourth tone syllable.

   yī → yí gè
   qī → qí gè
   bā → bá gè

"有"和"没有" ("Yǒu" hé "méiyǒu")

1. A: 李 老师 有 哥哥 吗?
   Lǐ ∘ ∘ yǒu gēge ∘?

   B: 有，他 有 一 个 哥哥。
   Yǒu, ∘ yǒu yí gè gēge.

2. A: 张 雷，你 有 哥哥 吗?
   Zhāng Léi, ∘ yǒu gēge ∘

   B: 有，我 有 一 个 哥哥。
   Yǒu, ∘ yǒu yí gè gēge.

   我 还 有 一 个 姐姐。
   ∘ hái yǒu yí gè jiějie.

3. A: 赵 建华，你 有 姐姐 吗?
   Zhào Jiànhuá, ∘ yǒu jiějie ∘?

   B: 没有，我 没有 姐姐，
   Méiyǒu, ∘ méiyǒu jiějie,

   我 只 有 一 个 妹妹。
   ∘ zhǐ yǒu yí gè mèimei.

Notes:

1. *Lǐ lǎoshī yǒu gēge ma? Yǒu, tā yǒu yí gè gēge* – Notice that the verb *yǒu* (有) is used in the answer much as one would say 'Yes, ...' in English. You can do this with other verbs as well, e.g.

Tā shì nǐ de péngyou ma?	***Shì**, tā shì wǒ de péngyou.*
*Tā **shàng** xiǎoxué ma?*	***Shàng**, tā shàng xiǎoxué.*
Tā yǒu gēge ma?	***Yǒu**, tā yǒu yí gè gēge.*

   If the answer is a negative one, i.e. 'No, ...', the verb is repeated in the negative, e.g.

*Tā **shàng** xiǎoxué ma?*	***Bú shàng**, tā bú shàng xiǎoxué.*
*Lǐ lǎoshī **yǒu** mèimei ma?*	***Méiyǒu**, tā méiyǒu mèimei.*
Tā shì nǐ de tóngxué ma?	***Bú shì**, tā bú shì wǒ de tóngxué.*

2. *Hái yǒu yí gè jiějie* – *Hái* (还) means 'also'. More examples:

Wǒ hái yǒu liǎng gè Rìběn péngyou.	I also have two Japanese friends.
Wǒmen hái xué Hànyǔ.	We also study Chinese.

3. Note that when you want to negate the verb *yǒu* (有), you must say ***méiyǒu*** (没有) not *bù yǒu.*

Nǐ	**yǒu**	gēge	**ma?**
Wǒ	**yǒu** méi **yǒu** zhǐ yǒu hái yǒu	gēge.	

兄弟姐妹 (Xiōngdì jiěmèi)

A: 阿伦 有 几 个 兄弟 姐妹?
Ālún yǒu jǐ gè xiōngdì jiěmèi?

B: 他 有 两 个 哥哥, 一 个 弟弟。
◦ yǒu liǎng gè gēge, yí gè dìdi.

他 没有 姐姐, 也 没有 妹妹。
◦ méiyǒu jiějie, ◦ méiyǒu mèimei.

请问，你 有 兄弟 姐妹 吗？
Qǐngwèn, ◦ yǒu xiōngdì jiěmèi ◦?

Find the Chinese →
该你了！**(Gāi nǐ le!)** →
Nǐ tīngdǒng le ma? →

说汉语二 (Shuō Hànyǔ Èr)

1. A: 张 雷，你 家 有 什么 人？
Zhāng Léi, ◦ jiā yǒu ◦ ◦ ◦?

B: 我 家 有 爸爸、妈妈、哥哥、
◦ jiā yǒu ◦ ◦, ◦ ◦, gēge,

姐姐 和 我。
jiějie hé ◦.

2. A: 赵 明，你 家 有 什么 人？
Zhào Míng, ◦ jiā yǒu ◦ ◦ ◦?

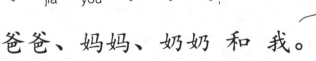

B: 我 家 有 四 个 人，
◦ jiā yǒu ◦ ◦ ◦,

爸爸、妈妈、奶奶 和 我。
◦ ◦, ◦ ◦, nǎinai hé ◦.

Find the Chinese

I also have an elder sister.
He has an elder brother.
How many brothers and sisters does Alan have?
I only have a younger sister.
Do you have any brothers and sisters?

该你了！(Gāi nǐ le!)

1. Find someone in your class who
   - has not got a younger brother
   - has not got any brothers or sisters
   - has an elder brother
   - has a younger brother
   - has not got any sisters
2. Conduct interviews in the class to find out how many brothers and sisters class members have. (All children living together in a family should be counted as brothers and sisters even if not fully related, e.g. half or step brothers and sisters.) Pool your results to make a graph of the numbers of *gēge*, *jiějie*, *mèimei* and *dìdi* to establish which is the largest category for your class.
   Remember to speak only Chinese during these activities!

你听懂了吗？

(Nǐ tīngdǒng le ma?)

1. a) Which is true?
   i) Mary has an elder brother and a sister.
   ii) Mary has only one brother.
   iii) Mary has two brothers and two sisters.

3. A: 阿伦，你呢？
Ālún, 。 。?

你家有什么人？
。 jiā yǒu 。 。 。?

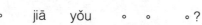

B: 我家有七个人，
。 jiā yǒu 。 。 。,

我爸爸、妈妈、

两个哥哥，一个弟弟，
liǎng gè gēge, yí gè dìdi.

一个妹妹和我。
yí gè mèimei hé 。.

Note:
When the pronouns *wǒ* (我), *nǐ* (你), *tā* (他), *wǒmen* (我们), *nǐmen* (你们), *tāmen* (她们) are used to describe a place to which one belongs, the *de* (的) is often omitted, for example:

wǒ de jiā		*wǒ jiā*
nǐ de jiā		*nǐ jiā*
tā de jiā	OR	*tā jiā*
wǒmen de xiǎoxué		*wǒmen xiǎoxué*
nǐmen de zhōngxué		*nǐmen zhōngxué*
tāmen de dàxué		*tāmen dàxué*

Nǐ **jiā**	**yǒu**	**shénme rén?**
Wǒ **jiā**	**yǒu**	bàba, māma, gēge, jiějie, dìdi, mèimei hé wǒ.

Find the Chinese →
该你了！**(Gāi nǐ le!)** →

LEARN TO READ page 61

LEARN TO WRITE Lesson 5 page 72

b) Before the conversation began
i) David was alone with Mary.
ii) David was alone with Yiping.
iii) David was with Yiping and her brother.

2. a) Which of these sentences is true?
i) Mary was not aware that Zhao Qing had a sister.
ii) Mary was aware that Zhao Qing had a sister.
iii) Mary was aware that Zhao Qing was the girl's younger sister.

b) Which is more probable?
i) Zhao Qing lives in Brisbane.
ii) Zhao Qing lives in Sydney.
iii) Zhao Qing lives somewhere other than Brisbane or Sydney.

Find the Chinese

How many people are there in your family?
In my family there's my father, my mother, my grandmother and myself.

该你了！ (Gāi nǐ le!)

Work in pairs, asking each other about your respective families. As one person describes his or her family, the other draws it (e.g. stick figures). When you both have completed your drawings, exchange them and check if you have understood each other correctly. Speak to each other only in Chinese!

2.3 I have a pet!

In the past, pets have not been very common in Chinese households, but as the standard of living improves, many families are now keeping pets. Birds and fish are the most common kinds of pets.

你们家养动物吗?

(Nǐmen jiā yǎng dòngwù ma?)

我们 家 养了 一 只 狗。
。 。 。 yǎngle 。 zhī gǒu.

它 叫 非非。
Tā 。 Fēifei.

我 养了 一 只 小 猫。
。 yǎngle 。 zhī 。 māo,

它 叫 咪咪。
Tā 。 Mīmi.

你们 家 养 动物 吗?
。 。 jiā yǎng dòngwù 。?

我们 家 不 养 动物。
。 。 jiā 。 yǎng dòngwù.

Notes:

1. *Wǒmen jiā yǎngle yì zhī gǒu* – *Le* (了) indicates that the action *yǎng* has happened.
2. *Gè* (个) which you have already learnt, is a general measure word which can be used with many nouns (see page 43). But there are other measure words which are used only with certain words or certain groups of words. *Zhī* (只) is one such measure word. It is used for some animals such as dogs, cats and birds.
3. *Tā* (它) means 'it' and is used when you are referring to animals or inanimate objects.

Here is how you ask someone if they have any pets, and the answers.

Nǐmen jiā	**yǎng**	**dòngwù**	ma?
Wǒmen jiā Wǒmen jiā	**yǎngle** **bù yǎng**	yì zhī gǒu. **dòngwù**	

When talking about animals you will need to use measure words. Here are some more common measure words for animals.

五 条 金鱼
。 tiáo jīnyú

两 只 鸟
。 zhī niǎo

几 匹 马?
。 pǐ mǎ?

My pet!

puppy 小狗 xiǎo gǒu
kitten 小猫 xiǎo māo
pony 小马 xiǎo mǎ
guinea pig 天竺鼠 tiānzhúshǔ
hamster 仓鼠 cāngshǔ
white mice 小老鼠 xiǎo lǎoshǔ
tortoise 乌龟 wūguī
sheep 绵羊 miányáng
lamb 小羊 xiǎo yáng
goat 山羊 shānyáng
snake 蛇 shé
budgie 虎皮鹦鹉 hǔpí yīngwǔ
lizard 蜥蜴 xīyì
frog 青蛙 qīngwā
beetle 甲虫 jiǎchóng
chicken 鸡 jī
chick 小鸡 xiǎo jī
duck 鸭 yā
duckling 小鸭 xiǎo yā
rabbit 兔子 tùzi

Class survey

Help the teacher write a list of pets on the blackboard. Write down (without showing anyone) your prediction of which pet is the most popular among the members of your class. Then, in small groups, ask each other what pets you have at home so that one person in the group can report back to the whole class while someone fills out the class profile on the blackboard. Finally, compare your own prediction with the results of the survey.

Remember to speak only Chinese throughout this activity!

My pet →
Class survey →

LEARN TO READ page 63

LEARN TO WRITE Lesson 6 page 74

2.4 Describing your pet

它真好看！ (Tā zhēn hǎokàn!)

狗
gǒu

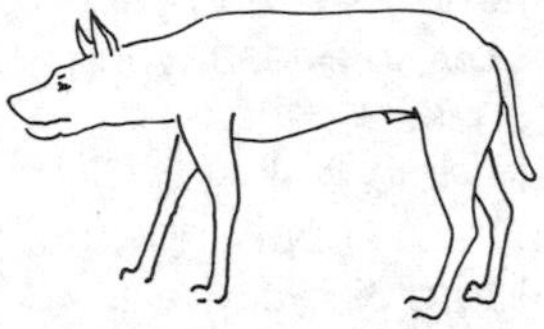

这 只 狗 很 大。
Zhèi ∘ ∘ hěn ∘

鱼
yú

这 条 鱼 很 小。
Zhèi tiáo yú hěn ∘.

羊
yáng

这 只 羊 挺 肥 的。
Zhèi ∘ yáng ∘ féi ∘.

猫
māo

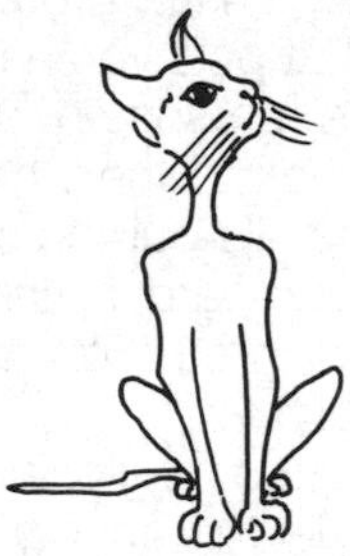

那 只 猫 真 瘦。
Nèi ∘ ∘ zhēn shòu.

鸟
niǎo

那 只 鸟 真 好看。
Nèi ∘ niǎo zhēn ∘ kàn.

小 狗
xiǎo gǒu

那 只 小狗 真 好玩儿。
Nèi ∘ ∘ ∘ zhēn ∘ wánr.

马
mǎ

那 匹 马 真 漂亮！
Nèi pǐ mǎ zhēn piàoliang!

小 猫
xiǎo māo

那 只 小 猫 真 淘气。
Nèi 。 。 。 zhēn táoqì.

Notes:

1. You have already learnt to use *zhè* (这) and *nà* (那) to express 'this', 'that', e.g.

This is Teacher Li.	*Zhè shì Lǐ lǎoshī.*
That is my friend.	*Nà shì wǒ de péngyou.*

   Note that in these sentences, *zhè* and *nà* represent the person or thing, i.e. 'this' = Teacher Li, and 'that' = my friend.

   Quite often 'this' and 'that' are used as 'pointer' to indicate the person or thing you are talking about, e.g. 'this schoolbag', 'that student'. *Zhè* and *nà* may also be used this way. *Zhè* and *nà* are usually pronounced as ***zhèi*** and ***nèi*** and generally a measure word is used, e.g.

this student	***zhèi****ge xuésheng*
that horse	***nèi*** *pǐ mǎ*

   When asking a question, you may use ***něi***.

Which kitten?	**Něi** *zhī xiǎo māo?*

2. *Féi* (肥) means 'fat' and is appropriate when used to describe an animal. When referring to a person, *pàng* (胖) is used instead.

大卫的狗 (Dàwèi de gǒu)

安娜： 它 真 高！
Ānnà: 。 zhēn gāo!

建华： 高？
Jiànhuá: Gāo?

他 不 高，他 挺 矮 的！
。 。 gāo, 。 。 ǎi 。!

安娜： 你 说 什么 呢？
Ānnà: ◦ shuō ◦ ◦ ◦?

建华： 我 说 大卫，他 挺 矮 的。
Jiànhuá: ◦ shuō Dàwèi, ◦ ◦ ǎi ◦.

安娜： 哦，我 以为 你 说 他 的
Ānnà: Ò, ◦ yǐwéi ◦ shuō ◦ ◦

狗 呢！
◦ ◦!

建华： 我们 不 说“狗 高”，
Jiànhuá: ◦ ◦ ◦ shuō "gǒu gāo"

我们 说“狗 大”。
◦ ◦ shuō "gǒu ◦".

安娜： 哦！他 的 狗 真 大。
Ānnà: Ò! ◦ ◦ ◦ zhēn ◦.

建华： 对！
Jiànhuá: Duì!

Notes:

1. Besides using *hěn* (很) when describing a pet, you may also say, for example:

zhēn *dà*	(真大)	really big
tǐng *dà de*	(挺大的)	quite big

You may also want to say:

bú *dà*	(不大)	not big

2. Note that *tǐng* … de (挺……的) is a phrase meaning 'quite …'; 'very …'; rather …'. Place your description between *tǐng* and *de*, e.g.

Běijīng tǐng dà de.
Zhāng Léi de jiějie tǐng hǎo de.
Tā de māo tǐng hǎowánr de.

3. The term *yǐwéi* (以为) means 'to think something *mistakenly*'. More examples:

   Wǒ yǐwéi shì nǐ de ne!
   Duìbuqǐ, wǒ yǐwéi nǐ shì Wáng lǎoshī.
   Wǒ yǐwéi nǐmen jiā yǎngle yì zhī gǒu.
   Tā yǐwéi nǐ shì wǒ de péngyou.

   What did the speakers in these examples misunderstand?

4. *Wǒ yǐwéi nǐ shuō tā de gǒu ne!* – *Ne* (呢) adds emphasis to the sentence.

5. In Chinese, animals are generally referred to as being big (*dà* 大), rather than tall (*gāo* 高) which explains the confusion in the above conversation. When you *read* the passage, however, you can see immediately that Anna and Jianhua are not talking about the same thing. Why is this so?

Find the Chinese →
Nǐ tīngdǒng le ma? →

Find the Chinese

What are you talking about?
We don't say a dog is 'tall', we say a dog is 'big'
I thought you meant his dog!.
That's right!

你听懂了吗?

(Nǐ tíngdǒng le ma?)

Which is true?

1. a) The cat belongs to the boy.
   b) It belongs to the girl.
   c) It belongs to someone else.
2. a) The boy doesn't like animals at all.
   b) He likes pets, irrespective of what they are.
   c) He prefers dogs to cats.

说汉语三 (Shuō Hànyǔ 3)

1. *(There is a knock on the front door.)*

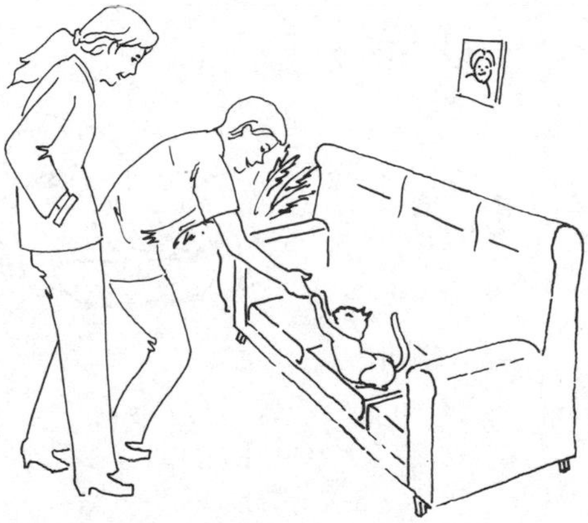

A: 谁 啊?
Shéi a?

B: 是 我, 马克。
。 。, Mǎkè.

A: 请 进, 请 进!
Qǐng jìn, qǐng jìn!

B: 哎哟, 这 只 猫 真 好玩儿!
Āiyō, 。 。 。 zhēn 。 wánr!

是 你 的 吗?

A: 不 是 我 的, 是 我 朋友 的。
。 。 。 。, 。 。 péngyou 。.

2. A: 你们 家 养 动物 吗?
　　∘ ∘ ∘ ∘ dòngwù ∘?

B: 养，我 养了 一 只 狗。

它 叫 非非，它 可 大 了!
Tā ∘ Fēifei, tā kě ∘ ∘!

我们 还 有 一 只 小 猫，叫 咪咪，
∘ ∘ hái ∘ ∘ ∘ ∘ ∘, ∘ Mīmi,

它 挺 淘气 的。
tā ∘ táoqì ∘.

A: 它们 打架 吗?
Tā ∘ dǎjià ∘?

B: 不，它们 不 打架，
∘, tā ∘ ∘ dǎjià.

它们 是 好 朋友。
Tā ∘ ∘ ∘ péngyou.

A: 真 有 意思!
Zhēn ∘ yìsi!

Notes:

1. When Mark says *Shì nǐ de ma?* he is referring to the cat. He could have said *Shì nǐ de* ***māo*** *ma?*, but because 'cat' is understood in the context, it is omitted. The same is true for *Bú shì wǒ de, shì wǒ péngyou de* in the dialogue.

2. *Tā kě dà le! — Kě … le* (可……了) *is an exclamatory sentence which emphasises the description. More examples:*

Tā kě piàoliang le!	How pretty it is!
Dàwèi de māo kě táoqì le!	David's cat is so naughty!

Find the Chinese →

Find the Chinese

Who's there?
It's not mine, it's my friend's.
No, they're good friends.
It's me, Mark.
We also have a kitten called Mimi.
How interesting!
Is it yours?
Do they fight?

My pet

In the boxes are sentences you can use to describe your pet.

Wǒmen jiā yǎngle	yì zhī māo. yì zhī gǒu yì zhī niǎo yì tiáo yú yì pǐ mǎ

Wǒmen jiā de gǒu māo niǎo'	hěn zhēn bù	dà. piàoliang	
	tǐng	xiǎo féi shòu	de.
	kě	hǎokàn hǎowánr táoqì	le!

该你了！(Gāi nǐ le!) →

LEARN TO READ page 64

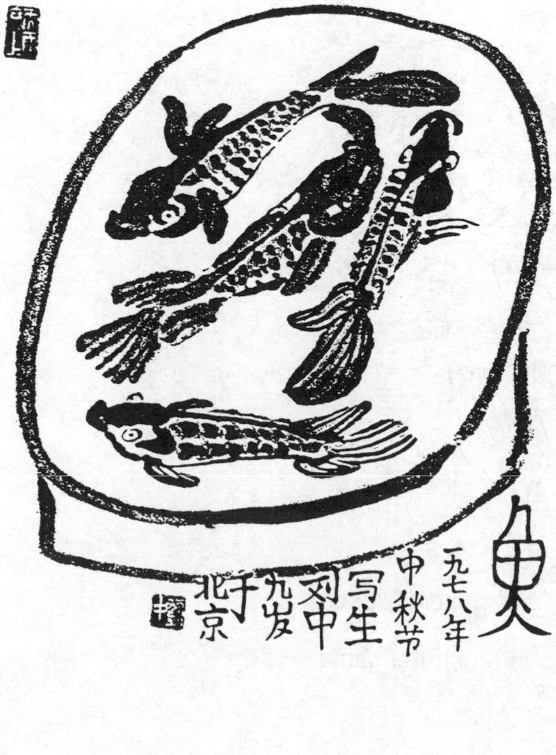

该你了！ (Gāi nǐ le!)

Draw a sketch of your favourite pet or bring a photo of it to class. Write a caption for your picture (using characters where you can) by combining a sentence from each of the boxes on the left side of the page, e.g.

Wǒmen jiā yǎngle yì pǐ mǎ.
Wǒmen jiā de mǎ zhēn piàoliang!

Pin your pictures and captions on the board for a display.

2.5 More counting: 11 to 99

多少? (Duōshao?)

Do you remember how to count to ten?
Here's how we say some of the numbers from 11 to 99. Can you read them out in Chinese?

11 十一
12 十二
13 十三
14 十四
15 十五
16 十六
17 十七
18 十八
19 十九

20 二十
21 二十一
⋮
30 三十
31 三十一
32 三十二
⋮
80 八十
81 八十一
82 八十二
⋮
99 九十九

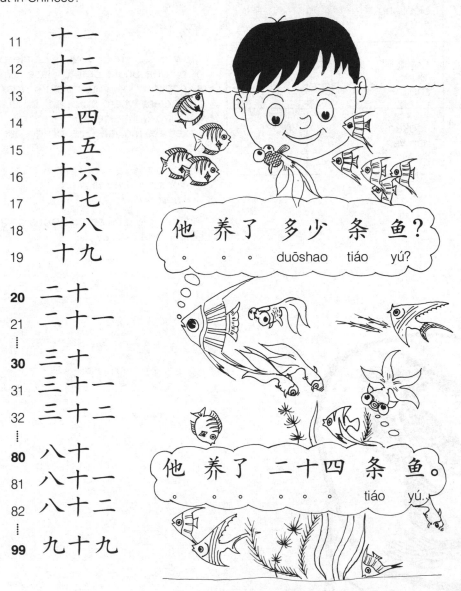

他 养了 多少 条 鱼?
。 。 。 duōshao tiáo yú?
他 养了 二十四 条 鱼。
。 。 。 。 。 。 tiáo yú.

Note:
You have learnt to use *jǐ* (几) when asking 'how many'. *Jǐ* is generally used when the numbers involved are quite small (under ten).

Duōshao (多少) also means 'how many' and is used in much the same way as *jǐ* (几) when you are talking about larger numbers.

练一练 (Liàn yí liàn)

Here is a tongue twister. Work out what it means first, then try to say one section at a time as fast as possible, then try to say the whole thing without stopping. The word *jiā* (加) means 'add' or 'plus', *jiǎn* (减) means 'subtract', and *háishi* (还是) means 'or'.

1. 四 是 四，十 是 十，
十四 是 十四，
四十 是 四十。

2. 十四 不 是 四十，
四十 不 是 十四。

3. 四 加 四十 是 四十四，
jiā
四十 加 四 也 是 四十四。

4. 十四 减 四，是 十 还是 四？
jiǎn háishi

Pass the number →

LEARN TO READ page 65

Pass the number!

Play 'Pass the message' with numbers. Divide into two or more large groups seated in circles. One person in each group writes down a secret number (greater than 10, but excluding the numbers 20, 30, 40, 50, 60, 70, 80, 90, 100). The same person then whispers the number (e.g. '47') to the person next to him or her who then whispers it to the next person and so on. When the last person in the circle is reached, he or she writes the number on the blackboard. The person who first whispered the number then writes that number beside it. See which group gets it right!

You can make the 'message' more complicated by making it consist of more than one figure (e.g. '47, 29, 88').

2.6 How old are you?

张 先生，您 多 大 了？

Zhāng xiānsheng, nín duō ∘ ∘?

我 三十五 岁 了。

∘ ∘ ∘ ∘ suì ∘.

王 老师，您 多 大 了？

Wáng ∘ ∘, nín duō ∘ ∘?

我 二十七 岁 了。

∘ ∘ ∘ ∘ suì ∘.

你 多 大 了？

∘ duō ∘ ∘?

我 十二 岁 了。

∘ ∘ ∘ suì ∘.

小朋友，你 几 岁 了？

∘ péngyou, ∘ ∘ suì ∘?

我 快 五 岁 了。

∘ kuài ∘ suì ∘.

王 太太 多 大 了?

Wáng tàitai duō ∘ ∘

她 快 四十 岁 了。

∘ kuài ∘ ∘ suì ∘

王 小姐 呢?

Wáng ∘ ∘ ∘?

我 不 知道。

∘ ∘ zhīdao.

Notes:

1. In traditional China great respect was accorded old age. It is therefore not considered impolite or prying to ask someone his or her age, even if you do not know that person very well. However, it is courteous to show the proper level of respect.

   When you are asking someone of your *own generation* or an *adult* his or her age, you say:

   Nǐ (or nín) ***duō dà le****?* (你/您多大了?)

   When you are asking a *child* his or her age, you may either say:

   Nǐ ***duō dà le****?* (你多大了?) or
   Nǐ ***jǐ suì le****?* (你几岁了?)

2. *Wǒ sānshíwǔ suì le* – *Le* (了) indicates that a change has taken place.

3. *Xiǎo péngyou* (小朋友) is a friendly way for a teenager or adult to address a small child.

4. Note that in Chinese, the title of the person follows the name.

Zhāng lǎoshī	Teacher Zhang
Lǐ Yún xiǎojie	Miss Li Yun
Wáng tàitai	Mrs Wang

5. *Tā kuài sìshí suì le* – *Kuài ... le* (快……了) means 'Nearly ...'. How would you say 'I'm nearly 15', 'Mark is nearly 24', 'My mother is nearly 38'?

Find the Chinese →
Nǐ tīngdǒng le ma? →
Which is not true? →

LEARN TO READ page 65

LEARN TO WRITE Lesson 7 page 75

Find the Chinese

How old is Mrs Wang?
I'm nearly five.
How old are you? *(speaking to a member of your class)*
How old are you? *(asking a child)*

你听懂了吗?

(Nǐ tīngdǒng le ma?)

Someone is being interviewed. Listen carefully to the conversation and jot down particulars about him, then see how many things you can say about him.

Which is not true?

Listen carefully to these people talking about themselves, their families and friends, then read the statements. There is one or more fact in each group which is untrue or not mentioned. Can you say which they are?

1. I'm Li Ming. I'm 13 years old and live with my father and mother in Beijing.
2. Anna is a great friend of mine. She's very tall.
3. My sister Jenny is teaching in Guangzhou at the moment. The rest of the family are living in Canberra. That's Mum, Dad, my elder brother and me.
4. My name is Mark. There are five in our family. I have two brothers. Both of them are in high school.
5. Mary and I both have a dog. Her dog is very naughty. Mine is one year old and she's beautiful!

学会认字 (Xuéhuì rèn zì)

2.1

Before reading the text, listen to the recording and answer the questions.

Dialogue:
True or false?
1. The boy was standing beside his parents and sister when Lin Fang arrived.
2. The boy and his sister are attending high school.
3. Lin Fang knows the boy very well.

Narration:
True or false?
1. Lin Fang's mother is not a teacher.
2. She attends high school.
3. Her sister also attends high school.

汉字表 (Hànzì biǎo)

			As in
这	zhè	*this*	这是……
爸	bà	*father*	爸爸
妈	mā	*mother*	妈妈
那	nà	*that*	那是……
妹	mèi	*younger sister*	妹妹
上	shàng	*to attend; on; previous*	上中学
小	xiǎo	*small*	小学

Text

1. 林方： 你好！

B: 你好！

(to his parents) 这是林方。

(to Lin Fang) 这是我爸爸，
这是我妈妈。

林方： 你们好！
妈妈： 你好！
爸爸： 你好！
B: 那是我妹妹。
林方： 你好！
妹妹： 你好！

(later on)
B: 我爸爸是老师。
我妈妈也是老师。
林方： 你妹妹呢？
B: 我妹妹上小学。

2. 你们好！我叫林方。这是我爸爸。这是我妈妈。那是我妹妹。

我爸爸是老师，妈妈也是老师。

我是学生。我妹妹也是学生。我上中学。她也上中学。

动动脑筋！

(Dòngdong nǎojīn!)

See if you can correctly guess what these words mean. They are made up of characters you know.

1. 小人
a) a small person
b) a short person
c) a mean person

2. 小名
a) a short name
b) a pet name
c) a name of a child

2.2

Before reading the text, listen to the recording and answer the questions.

True or false?
1. The boy has two sisters.
2. The boy also has a brother.
3. The girl is the youngest member of her family.

汉字表 (Hànzì biǎo)

			As in
一	yī	*one*	
二	èr	*two*	
三	sān	*three*	
四	sì	*four*	
五	wǔ	*five*	
六	liù	*six*	
七	qī	*seven*	
八	bā	*eight*	
九	jiǔ	*nine*	
十	shí	*ten*	
有	yǒu	*to have*	
几	jǐ	*how many*	几个?
个	gè	*(measure word)*	
兄	xiōng	*elder brother*	兄弟
弟	dì	*younger brother*	弟弟
姐	jiě	*elder sister*	姐姐
两	liǎng	*two (of something)*	两个人
哥	gē	*elder brother*	哥哥
没	méi	*not*	没有
和	hé	*and*	他和我

动动脑筋!

(Dòngdong nǎojīn!)

Guess what these words mean. They are made up of characters you know.

1. 三三两两
   a) three thousand three hundred and twenty-two
   b) three of one thing and two of another
   c) a description of people gathered in groups of two's and three's

2. 大哥
   a) big brother
   b) elder brother
   c) eldest brother

3. 大姐
   a) elder sister
   b) big sister
   c) eldest sister

Text

1. 一 二 三 四 五 六 七 八 九 十

2. G: 你有几个兄弟姐妹？

 B: 我有一个姐姐和一个妹妹。

 你呢？

 G: 我有两个哥哥。

 我没有姐姐，

 也没有弟弟和妹妹。

2.3

Before reading the text, listen to the recording and answer the questions.

True of false?
1. Both the boy and girl have pet dogs at home.
2. Lili is the name of the cat.
3. The girl keeps a cat and two large dogs as pets.

汉字表 (Hànzì biǎo)

			As in
家	jiā	home; family	我的家
养	yǎng	ro raise; bring up	养狗
狗	gǒu	dog	一只狗
了	le	(aspect particle)	养了一只猫
只	zhī	(measure word)	一只狗
猫	māo	cat	一只猫

Text

B: 我们家养了一只猫。

G: 是吗？你们家的猫叫什么名字？

B: 利利。

 你们家也养猫吗？

G: 我们家不养猫，

 我们家养了两只狗。

猜一猜！

(Cāi yi cāi!)

Cāi yi cāi means to 'have a guess'. See if you can guess what these words might mean. They are made up of characters you know.

1. Someone described as

 # 不三不四
 a) is not three or four years old
 b) is a shady character
 c) does not have three or four ✓ of something

2. # 一家人
 a) a family
 b) a house full of people

3. # 国家
 a) a country where one is living
 b) countries and homes ✓
 c) nation

2.4

Before reading the text, listen to the recording and answer the questions.

True or false?
1. The boy has never seen the dog before.
2. The girl has a beautiful dog.

汉字表 (Hànzì biǎo)

			As in
请	qǐng	*please; ask*	请进！
进	jìn	*to enter*	
谁	shéi	*who*	谁的
真	zhēn	*real, true*	真好看
看	kàn	*to see, look, watch, read*	好看

Text

(There is a knock on the door. The girl opens the door)

G: 大同！
大同： 你好吗？
G: 挺好的，你呢？
大同： 也挺好的。
G: 请进，请进！

大同： 这只狗真好看！
这是谁的狗？
G: 是我的。

猜一猜！

(Cāi yi cāi!)

See if you can guess what this word means.

小看

1. to peek
2. to look for a short while
3. to belittle

2.5

Before reading the text, listen to the recording and write down the numbers you hear.

十一	四十五	六十七
八十九	九十二	七十
八十三	七十一	六十四
五十五	二十三	十四

2.6

Before reading the text, listen to the recording and answer the questions.

True or false?
1. The speaker's surname is Sheng.
2. He has a brother who is much older than he is.
3. He has no sisters at all.
4. They have a cat and a dog at home.

汉字表 (Hànzì biǎo)

			As in
同	tóng	*same; together*	同学
王	wáng	*surname*	王老师
岁	suì	*years old, age*	几岁?
北	běi	*north*	北京
京	jīng	*capital* (as in *Běijīng*)	
住	zhù	*to live*	住北京
对	duì	*towards; correct*	对不起
还	hái	*still, also*	还有

Text

老师好，同学们好！我叫王汉生。我十二岁。我住北京。

动动脑筋！

(Dòngdong nǎojīn!)

See if you can guess what these words might mean. They are made up of characters you know.

1. Compared with you, if someone is
   同岁
   he or she is …

2. 大小
   a) size (of something)
   b) big or small
   c) a big version of the character 小

3. 大人
   a) a giant
   b) an adult person
   c) somebody who is big and strong

4. 有名
   a) has been given a name
   b) in possession of someone else's name
   c) is well-known or famous

5. A person said to be
   没大没小
   a) is neither big nor small
   b) shows no respect for his or her elders
   c) does not know the difference between the characters 大 and 小.

我家有爸爸、妈妈、哥哥和我四个人。我没有姐姐，弟弟和妹妹。我爸爸是老师，妈妈也是老师。我和哥哥是学生。哥哥上大学，我上中学。

对了，我们家还养了一只狗和一只猫！

Note:
Duì le, ... – Duì le (对了) indicates that the speaker has suddenly remembered something.

Summary

2.1 Meet my family

Now you can:

introduce members of your family or a friend:
Zhè shì wǒ bàba. 这是我爸爸。
Zhè shì wǒ jiějie Zhào Yún. 这是我姐姐赵云。
Nà shì wǒ mèimei. 那是我妹妹。
Zhè shì Mǎdīng. 这是马丁。
Zhè shì wǒ de péngyou Huāzǐ. 这是我的朋友花子。
Zhè shì tā dìdi. 这是她弟弟。

describe where someone goes to school:
Tā shàng xiǎoxué. 他上小学。
Tā shàng zhōngxué. 她上中学。
Tā shì dàxuéshēng. 他是大学生。

say where you live:
Wǒ zhù Guǎngzhōu. 我住广州。

ask where someone lives:
Tā zhù nǎr? 他住哪儿?

Useful expressions
Wǒ lái jièshào yíxià ... 我来介绍一下...... *Let me introduce you ...*

Grammar and usage reference
Grandparents, different terms for page 38
Chinese names page 39
De (的) in *wǒ de* (我的), *nǐ de* (你的) *tā de* (他的), omitted when describing family relationships page 39
Japanese names in Chinese page 41
Zhù (住) page 42
Australian capitals page 42

2.2 My family

Now you can:

count to 10:
Yī, èr, sān, sì, wǔ, liù, qī, bā, jiǔ, shí. 一，二，三，四，五，六，七，八，九，十。

ask how many brothers or sisters someone has:
Nǐ yǒu gēge ma? 你有哥哥吗?
Nǐ yǒu jǐ gè xiōngdì jiěmèi? 你有几个兄弟姐妹?
(Qǐngwèn,) nǐ yǒu xiōngdì jiěmèi ma? (请问,) 你有兄弟姐妹吗?

possible replies:
Wǒ yǒu liǎng gè gēge, yí gè dìdi. 我有两个哥哥，一个弟弟。
Wǒ yǒu yí gè gēge, hái yǒu yí gè jiějie. 我有一个哥哥，还有一个姐姐。
Wǒ méiyǒu jiějie. 我没有姐姐。
Wǒ zhǐ yǒu yí gè mèimei. 我只有一个妹妹。

answer a question affirmatively or negatively:
Q. Lǐ lǎoshī yǒu gēge ma? 李老师有哥哥吗?
A: Yǒu, tā yǒu yí gè gēge.. 有，他有一个哥哥。

Q. Zhào Jiànhuá, nǐ yǒu jiějie ma? 赵建华，你有姐姐吗?
A. Méiyǒu, wǒ méiyǒu jiějie. 没有，我没有姐姐。

ask what people there are in someone's family:
Nǐ jiā yǒu shénme rén? 你家有什么人?

possible reply:
Wǒ jiā yǒu bàba, māma, nǎinai hé wǒ. 我家有爸爸、妈妈、奶奶和我。

Grammar and usage reference
Gè (个) measure word page 43
Nouns in Chinese generally have no plural form page 43
Liǎng (两) used for 'two' when followed by a measure word page 44
Yī (一) *qī* (七) *bā* (八) pronounced in second tone page 44
Use of verb to answer 'Yes' or 'No'. page 45
Hái (还) adverb meaning 'also'. page 45
Méi (没) used to negate *yǒu* (有) page 45
De (的) often omitted after *wǒ* (我), *nǐ* (你), *tā* (他) when describing a place to which one belongs page 47

2.3 I have a pet!

Now you can:

ask someone if he or she has a pet:
Nǐmen jiā yǎng dòngwù ma? 你们家养动物吗?

reply when you are asked if you have a pet:
Wǒmen jiā yǎngle yì zhī māo. 我们家养了一只猫。
Wǒmen jiā bù yǎng dòngwù. 我们不养动物。

Grammar and usage reference
Le (了) indicating that the action of the verb has happened page 49
Zhī (只) measure word page 49
Tā (它) page 49

Vocabulary reference
Pets page 49

2.4 Describing your pet

Now you can:

describe your own or someone else's pet:
Zhèi tiáo yú hěn xiǎo. 这条鱼很小。
Nèi zhī xiǎo gǒu zhēn hǎowánr. 那只小狗真好玩儿。
Wǒmen jiā de māo tǐng táoqì de. 我们家的猫挺淘气的。

say you thought something mistakenly:
Wǒ yǐwéi nǐ shuō tā de gǒu ne! 我以为你说他的狗呢!

describe ownership:
Bú shì wǒ de, shì wǒ péngyou de. 不是我的，是我朋友的。

Useful expressions
Āiyō! (哎哟!) (*exclamation expressing surprise*)
Zhēn yǒu yìsi! (真有意思!) *How interesting!*
Duì. (对) *That's right*.

Grammar and usage reference
Zhèi (这) and *nèi* (那) page 51
Féi (肥) used for animals, not *páng* (胖) page 51
Hěn (很), *zhēn* (真), *bù* (不) used in descriptions page 52
Tǐng ... de (挺……的) page 52
Yǐwéi (以为) meaning 'to think mistakenly' page 53
Ne (呢) adds emphasis to the sentence page 53
Gāo (高) not used to describe animals page 53
Omission of noun following pronouns with *de*, e.g. *wǒ de* (我的), *nǐ de* (你的), *tā de* (他的) etc if understood in context page 54
Kě ... le (可……了) as an exclamatory sentence page 54
Describing a pet page 55

2.5 More counting 11 to 99

Now you can:

count from 11 to 99:
shíyī ... jiǔshíjiǔ 十一……九十九

express addition or subtraction:
Sì jiā sìshí shì sìshísì. 四加四十是四十四。
Shísì jiǎn sì shì shí. 十四减四是十。

Grammar and usage reference
Jǐ (几) and *duōshao* (多少) page 56

2.6 How old are you?

Now you can:

ask someone how old he or she is:
Nǐ duō dà le? 你多大了？
Zhāng xiānsheng, nín duō dà le? 张先生，您多大了？
Xiǎopéngyou, nǐ jǐ suì? 小朋友，你几岁？

possible replies:
Wǒ èrshíqī suì le. 我二十七岁了。
Wǒ kuài wǔ suì le. 我快五岁了。

Grammar and usage reference
Asking someone's age page 59
Le （了） indicating a change page 59
Title follows name page 59
Kuài ... le （快……了） page 59

LEARN TO READ

Useful expressions
Duì le, ... （对了，……） *That's right, ...* (on remembering something)
Duì le! （对了！） *That's right!*

学会写字 第四课 (Xuéhuì xiě zì Dì-sì ke)

汉字表 (Hànzì biǎo)

Basic stroke

As in

妈

这	zhè *this*	的	de *(structural particle)*
爸	bà *father*	妈	mā *mother*
上	shàng *to attend; on; previous*	中	zhōng *middle*

Text

这是我爸爸、妈妈。
我爸爸是老师。
我妈妈也是老师。
我是学生。
我上中学。

学会写字 第五课 (Xuéhuì xiě zì Dì-wǔ kè)

汉字表 (Hànzì biǎo)

Basic stroke

As in

九

一	yī *one*	二	èr *two*
三	sān *three*	四	sì *four*

五	wǔ *five*	六	liù *six*
七	qī *seven*	八	bā *eight*
九	jiǔ *nine*	十	shí *ten*

Text

一 二 三 四 五

六 七 八 九 十

学会写字 第六课 (Xuéhuì xiě zì Dì-liù kè)

汉字表 (Hànzì biǎo)

家	jiā *home, family*	有	yǒu *to have*
妹	mèi *younger sister*	和	hé *and*
几	jǐ *how many*	个	gè (*measure word*)

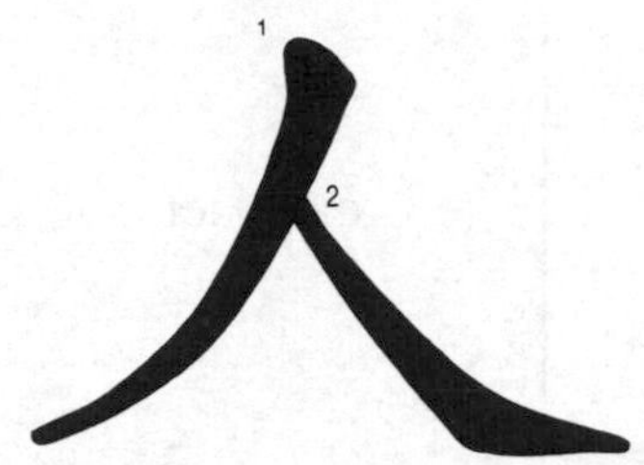

rén *person*

Text

1. A: 你家有几个人？
   B: 我家有四个人，爸爸、妈妈、妹妹和我。

2. 这是我爸爸。
   这是我妈妈。
   这是我妹妹。

学会写字 第七课 (Xuéhuì xiě zì Dì-qī kè)

汉字表 (Hànzì biǎo)

Basic stroke

As in

岁	岁 没

suì *years old*

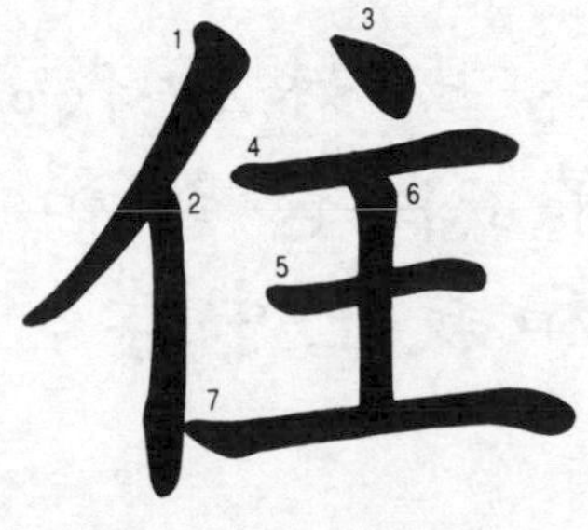

zhù *to live*

姐	jiě *elder sister*	没	méi *not*
哥	gē *elder brother*	弟	dì *younger brother*
小	xiǎo *small*		

Text

你们好！我叫小生。我十四岁。我住……

我家有五个人，爸爸，妈妈、姐姐、妹妹和我。我没有哥哥和弟弟。我爸爸和妈妈是老师。姐姐和我上中学，妹妹上小学。

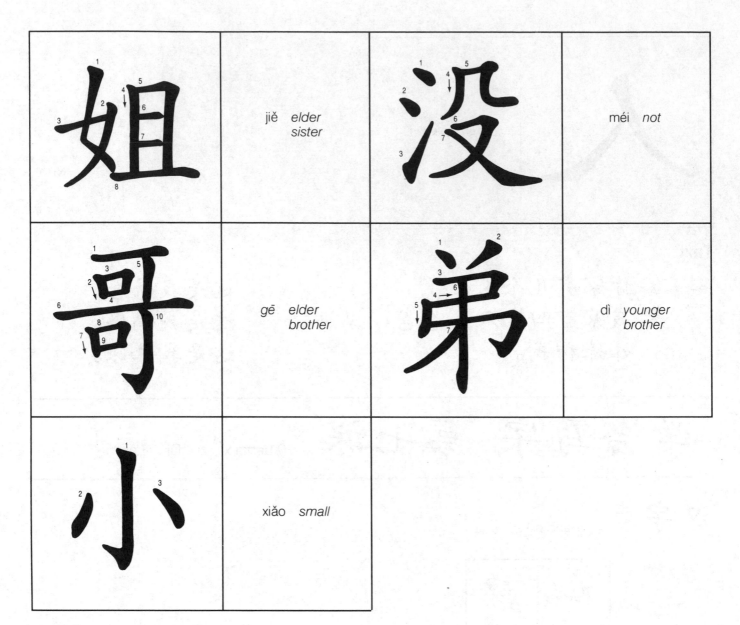

UNIT 3 Our Classroom

第三单元
Dì-sān dānyuán

上课了！
Shàngkè le!

In this unit you will learn how to talk about your classroom, how to say which things belong to which people and how to ask your teacher questions. You will also learn how to say the date and how to wish someone 'Happy Birthday!'.

3.1 Our classroom

我是林兰兰 (Wǒ shì Lín Lánlán)

Lanlan is a typical high school student. She lives at home with her family and goes to school each day. That's six days a week because in China, Saturday is a school day too! Lanlan catches the local bus (there are no 'school' buses to school). Sometimes she goes by bicycle.

At a Chinese high school, members of one class have their own classroom and stay together for most of their lessons, so all the students in the class get to know each other very well and many close friendships are formed within the group.

Look carefully at classroom. You will see a lot of familiar objects there – desks, schoolbags etc. Do you think Lanlan's classroom is like yours? In what ways is it the same? In what ways is it different?

我 叫 林 兰兰。
∘ ∘ Lín Lánlán.

这 是 我 的 家。
∘ ∘ ∘ ∘ jiā.

这 是 我 的 房间。
∘ ∘ ∘ ∘ fángjiān.

这 是 我 的 学校。
∘ ∘ ∘ ∘ ∘ xiào.

这 是 我们的 教室。
∘ ∘ ∘ ∘ ∘ jiàoshi.

这 是 我 的 桌子。
∘ ∘ ∘ ∘ zhuōzi.

这 是 我 的 书包。
◦ ◦ ◦ ◦ shūbāo.

那 是 王 华。
Nà ◦ ◦ Huá.

她 是 我 的 好 朋友。
◦ ◦ ◦ ◦ ◦ péngyou.

那 是 黄 老师。
Nà ◦ Huáng ◦ ◦.

黄 老师 是 我们 的 英语 老师。
Huáng ◦ ◦ ◦ ◦ ◦ ◦ Yīng ◦ ◦ ◦.

LEARN TO READ page 98

LEARN TO WRITE Lesson 8 page 109

3.2 Whose is it?

谁的？ (Shéi de?)

All these things belong to someone. Find out who they belong to.

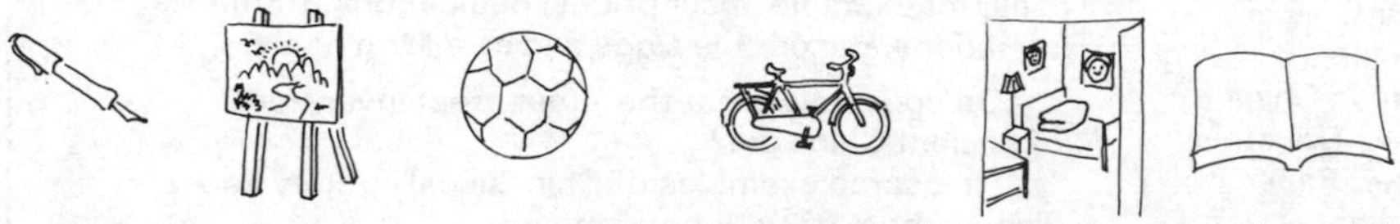

笔	画(儿)	球	自行车	房间	书
bǐ	huà(r)	qiú	zìxíngchē	fángjiān	shū

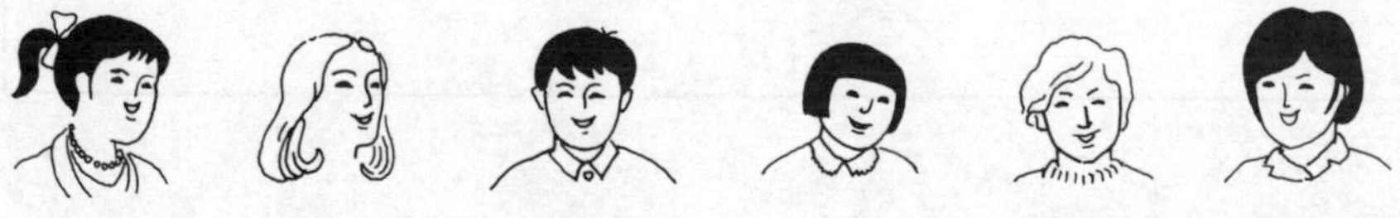

Lín Fāng	Ānnà	Jiànhuá	Lánlán	Bǐdé	lǎoshī

	Zhè shì Nà	**Lín Lánlán de** shū ma?
Shì Bú shì,	zhè shì nà zhè bú shì nà	**Lín Lánlán de** (shū). **Lín Lánlán de** (shū).

你听懂了吗?

(Nǐ tīngdǒng le ma?)

Which is true?

1. The boy gave Judy his pen.
2. The boy gave Judy Anna's pen.
3. They boy gave Judy her pen.

Nǐ tīngdǒng le ma? →

说汉语一 (Shuō Hànyǔ 1)

劳拉: 我 捡到 一 支 笔,
Láolā: ◦ jiǎndào ◦ zhī bǐ,

你 知道 是 谁 的 吗?

大卫: 我 不 知道。
Dàwèi:

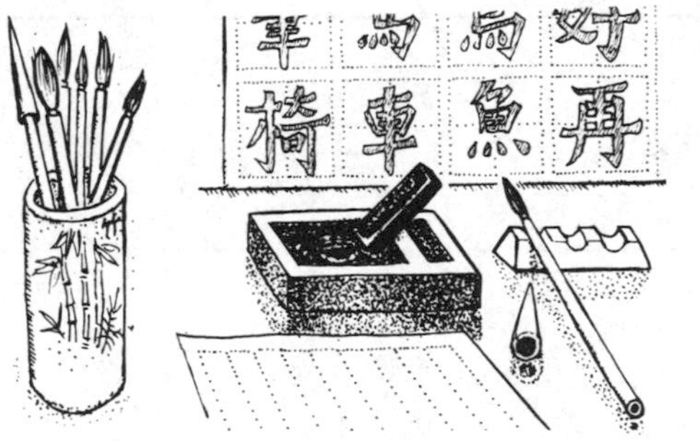

Bǐ can mean any kind of writing instrument — pen, pencil, ball point pen or Chinese writing brush.

The writing brush is traditionally regarded in China as one of the "four treasures of the studio". The other three are the inkslab, the inkstone and paper. Paper is one of the "four great inventions" of ancient China where it was in use several centuries earlier than it was in Europe.

Writing has always been held in special esteem in China. Calligraphy (beautiful handwriting, almost always done with a brush), is regarded as an art form in its own right. Examples of beautifully written characters, often in the form of a quotation from some famous work, are hung on the walls of people's homes just as paintings of scenery are, and great calligraphers take their place in the history of Chinese art alongside great artists.

But people in China today do not go around with writing brushes and inkstones in their pockets! Although schoolchildren still learn to write with a brush, for everyday use, at school and at work, fountain pens and ball point pens are used. Brush writing today is reserved for special occasions and uses, for example: inscriptions, dedications, formal invitations, decorative signs and as a form of art.

*Do you know what the "four great inventions" of ancient China are?

*Find some examples of Chinese calligraphy and display them on your noticeboard.

马丁： 我看看，…… 哦，是安娜的。
Mǎdīng: 。 kànkan, … Ò, 。 Ānnà 。

劳拉： 安娜，这是你的笔吗？
Láolā: Ānnà, 。 。 。 。 bǐ 。?

安娜： 哦，是我的。
Ānnà: Ò, 。 。 。

我以为它丢了呢！
。 yǐwéi tā diū 。 。!

劳拉： 给你。
Láolā: Gěi 。

安娜： 谢谢你！
Ānnà: Xièxie 。!

劳拉： 不谢。
Láolā: 。 xiè.

Notes:

1. When Martin says to Laura "Wǒ **kànkan** …" he is saying that he will look at the pen to see if he knows who it belongs to. By repeating the verb *kàn* (看) Martin indicates the action is fairly brief and casual and softens the tone of the sentence.
2. *Wǒ yǐwéi tā diū le ne!* – *diū le* (丢了) means that something has been lost or is missing.
3. It is courteous to make a polite response when someone says 'Thank you' to you, so when Anna says *Xièxie nǐ* (谢谢你) to Laura, she replies **Bú xiè** (不谢). Another polite response to *Xièxie* is **Búyòng kèqi** (不用客气) or just **Bú kèqi** (不客气). Equivalent responses in English would be 'Don't mention it', 'Not at all' or 'That's OK.'

谢谢！
Xièxie!
不用客气。
Búyòng kèqi.

Find the Chinese →
这是谁的？ →

LEARN TO READ page 99

LEARN TO WRITE Lesson 9 page 110

Find the Chinese

Let me have a look ...
Is this your pen?
I picked up a pen.
It's Anna's.
It's mine.
Here you are. (*giving something to someone*)
Please don't mention it. (*polite response*)
I thought it was lost.

这是谁的？

The class divides into two groups. Each group gathers a number of objects belonging to members of its group. (Large objects could be represented by a drawing, with the owner's name on the back.) One person from each group takes it in turn to hold up the objects belonging to his/her group and asks whose it is and the members of the other group guess or say who the owner is (no more than three guesses). The actual owners should not reveal themselves unless the other group fails to guess the correct owner, in which case that group loses a point.

3.3 How do you say it?

这叫什么？ (Zhè jiào shénme?)

这 叫 书包。
。 。 shūbāo.

请问，这 叫 什么？

桌子
zhuōzi

椅子
yǐzi

黑板
hēibǎn

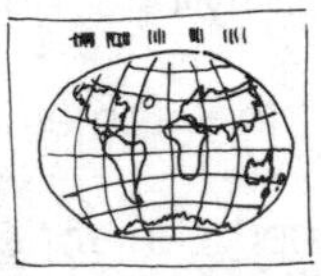

地图
dìtú

HANYU 1
STUDENT'S

课本
kèběn

练习本

练习本
liànxíběn

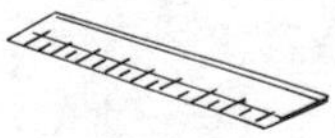

尺子
chǐzi

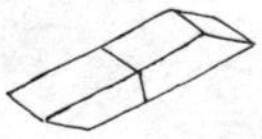

橡皮
xiàngpí

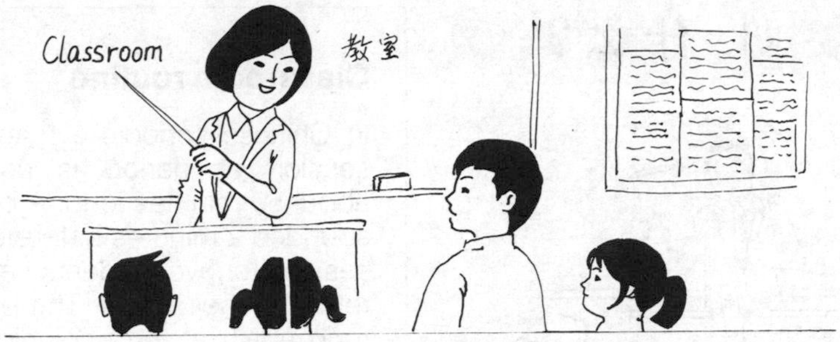

王华： 老师，“教室”英文 叫 什么？

∘ Huá: ∘ ∘, “jiàoshì” Yīngwén ∘ ∘ ∘?

黄 老师：“教室” 英文 叫 “classroom”.

Huáng ∘ ∘: “Jiàoshì” Yīngwén ∘

安娜： 老师，“Map of China” 中文 怎么 说？

Ānnà: ∘ ∘, ∘ wén zěnme shuō?

老师： 中国 地图。

∘ ∘: ∘ ∘ dìtú.

我知道！ (Wǒ zhīdao!)

马克： 老师，“exercise book” 中文 怎么 说？

Mǎkè: ∘ ∘ ∘ wén zěn ∘ shuō?

老师： “Exercise book” 中文 叫 “练习本”。

∘ ∘: ∘ wén ∘ “liànxíběn”.

马克： 哦。

Mǎkè: Ò.

Hànyǔ, Zhōngguóhuà and **Zhōngwén**

Hànyǔ, (汉语) refers to the language as a whole as well as the spoken form.

Zhōngwén (中文) refers mainly to the written form of the language and its literature.

Huà (话) means ‘speech’ or ‘talk’, so when you say 中国话 you are referring to the spoken form of the Chinese language.

老师： 我们的 "Student's Book" 叫 什么？

马克： 我 知道！
Mǎkè:

"Student's Book" 叫 "学生本"！
○ " ○ ○ běn"!

老师： 不 对，这 是 你们 的 "课本"。
○ ○: ○ duì, ○ ○ ○ ○ ○ "kèběn".

马克： 哦？！
Mǎkè: Ó?!

老师： 大家 懂 了 吗？
○ ○: ○ ○ dǒng ○ ○?

大家： 懂 了。
○ ○: Dǒng ○

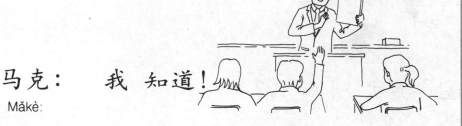

老师： 下课！
○ ○: Xiàkè!

Find the Chinese →

Classroom routine

In Chinese schools a teaching session or period is usually about 50 minutes long. A bell is sounded 2 minutes before each session to give students time to return to their seats. The bell is rung again at the beginning of the period.

As the teacher walks into the classroom the class monitor calls out *"Qǐlì"* (起立！) ('Stand up!'). The students rise to their feet, and remain so until the teacher says *"Zuòxia!"* (坐下！) ('Be seated!').

A student who is late is expected to announce his or her arrival by opening the door and calling out "*Bàogào!*" (报告！) ('Reporting!'). The teacher gives permission to join the class by saying "*Jìnlai*" (进来) which is often followed by a request for an explanation of the student's lateness.

Students are expected to sit upright and be attentive throughout the session. To ask the teacher a question during the session, the student will raise his or her forearm with elbow touching the desk or at desk level.

A bell signals the end of each session. When ready, the teacher will usually indicate that the session is over by saying *"Xiàkè"* (下课) ('Class dismissed') upon which everyone stands up. Unless told that they may leave the room, students wait until the teacher leaves the classroom before going out themselves.

Find the Chinese

Does everyone understand?
That's not right.
How do you say 'classroom' in English?
Class dismissed!
I know!

1
"练习本" 英文 叫 "exercise book".
"Liànxíběn" Yīngwén 。
2.
李明！
Lǐ Míng!
3.
请 您 再 说 一 遍。
Qǐng nín zài shuō yí biàn.

Nǐ tīngdǒng le ma? →
Vocabulary bee →

LEARN TO READ page 100

你听懂了吗?

(Nǐ tīngdǒng le ma?)

Which is true?

1. a) Only the girl keeps a pet.
   b) Only the boy has a pet.
   c) Both the girl and boy keep pets.
2. a) *Lǎoshǔ* means 'hamster' in English.
   b) *Lǎoshǔ* means 'rat'.
   c) *Lǎoshǔ* does not mean 'hamster' or 'rat'.

Vocabulary bee

Divide into teams and hold a 'Vocabulary bee'. The questions could be about actual objects (e.g. *Zhè Zhōngwén jiào shénme?*) or words or phrases (e.g. *'Thank you' Zhōngwén zěnme shuō?*) but they must be based on vocabulary which has been encountered in class.

3.4 Which one is it?

这些东西是谁的?

(Zhèixiē dōngxi shì shéi de?)

1. A: 这个 书包 是 谁 的?
   Zhèige shūbāo 。 。 。?

   B: 是 林兰兰 的。
   。 。 Lánlán 。

2. A: 这些 东西 是 谁 的?
   Zhèixiē dōngxi 。 。 。?

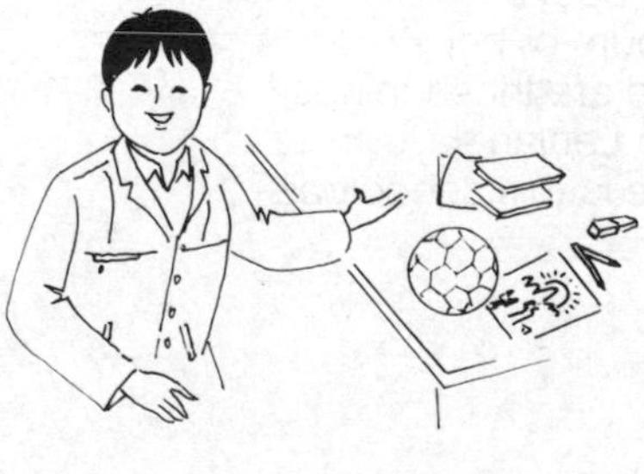

   B: 那些 书 是 李明 的。
   Nèixiē shū 。 Lǐ Míng 。

   这些 东西 是 我 的。
   Zhèixiē dōngxi 。 。 。

这个还是那个? (Zhèige háishi nèige?)

A: 这 块 橡皮 是
Zhèi kuài xiàngpí ∘

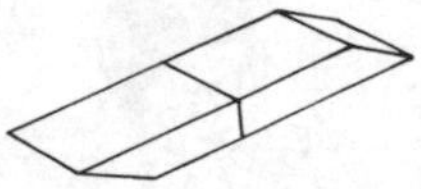

林兰兰 的 还是 李明 的?
∘ Lánlán ∘ ∘ ∘ Lǐ Míng ∘?

B: 我 不 知道。

那个 球 是 你 的 还是 她 的?
Nèi ∘ qiú ∘ ∘ ∘ ∘ ∘ ∘ ∘?

那 张 画儿 是 阿伦 的 还是 大卫 的?
Nèi zhāng huàr ∘ Ālún ∘ ∘ ∘ Dàwèi ∘?

请问,"课本" 英文 是 "exercise book"
∘ ∘, ∘ ∘ Yīng ∘ ∘
还是 "textbook"?

Notes:

1. *Zhèixiē dōngxi shì shéi de? – if there is more than one person or thing, we use the measure word* ***xiē*** (些). For example:

THESE students	***zhèixiē*** *xuésheng*
THOSE books	***nèixiē*** *shū*
WHICH paintings?	***Něixiē*** *huàr?*

2. When the person or thing you are referring to is *already understood* by the listener, you may drop the noun (the person or thing), e.g. the answer to the question

   Něi běn shū shì nǐ de? Which book is yours?

   could be answered by either

   a) *Zhèi běn shū shì wǒ de.* This book is mine.
   or
   b) *Zhèi běn shì wǒ de.* This one is mine.

Find the Chinese →

Find the Chinese

I don't know.
Those books
Is it yours or her's?
Whose are these things?
It's Lin Lanlan's.
Whose is this schoolbag?

Here is a list of nouns you have learnt and their measure words (MW):

MW	Nouns
个 gè	老师，学生，同学，人， 中国人，朋友，哥哥， péngyou 姐姐，弟弟，妹妹 东西，书包，球 dōngxi shūbāo qiú 学校，小学，中学， 教室，房间 jiàoshì fángjiān
把 bǎ	椅子，尺子 yǐzi chǐzi
本	书，课本，练习本 shū liànxí 。
块 kuài	黑板，橡皮 hēibǎn xiàngpí
辆 liàng	自行车 zìxíngchē

匹 pǐ	马 mǎ
条 tiáo	鱼，狗 yú
张 zhāng	桌子，地图，画儿 zhuōzi dìtú huàr
支 zhī	笔
只	动物，羊，狗，猫，鸟 dòngwù yáng niǎo

借(给)我，好吗？

(Jiè(gěi) wǒ, hǎo ma?)

1. A: 这 本 书 是 你 的 还是 赵 云 的？
   Zhèi běn shū 。 。 。 。 。 Zhào Yún 。?

   B: 是 赵 云 的。
   。 Zhào Yún 。.

   A: 赵 云，这 是 你 的 书 吗？
   Zhào Yún, 。 。 。 。 shū 。?

   C: 是。

   A: 借(给) 我 看看，好 吗？
   Jiè (。) 。 。 。, 。 。?

C: 好。

2\. A: 这是你的小说吗？

B: 是我的。

A: 借（给）我一本，好吗？
Jiè (。) 。 。 。, 。 。?

B: 好，你要哪本？
。 。 yào 。 。?

A: 我要这本。
。 yào zhèi 。

B: 那本书可好看了！
Nèi 。 shū kě 。 。 。!

Note:
Nǐ yào něi běn? — As 'novel' is understood, the word *xiǎoshuō* may be omitted.

A: 要 哪个？
Yào něige?
B: 要……这个。
Yào ... zhèige.

To sum up (with 'pictures' and 'books'):

this picture that book whick picture?	***zhèi** zhāng huàr* ***nèi** běn shū* ***Něi** zhāng huàr?*
these pictures those books Which pictures?	*zhèi**xiē** huàr* *nèi**xiē** shū* *Něi**xiē** huàr?*

Find the Chinese

Could I borrow it to read?
Which one would you like?
Could I borrow one?
All right. *(agreeing to a request)*
That's a really good book!
I'd like this one.

Find the Chinese →

LEARN TO READ page 101

3.5 What's the date today?

今天是几月几号? (Jīntiān shì jǐ yuè jǐ hào?)

1. 哪 年?
Něi nián?

一九九三年。
Yī jiǔ jiǔ sān nián.

2. 几 月?
Jǐ yuè?

四月。
Sìyuè.

1993 APRIL

SUN	MON	TUE	WED	THUR	FRI	SAT
				1	2	3
4	5	6	7	8	9	10
11	12	13	14	15	16	17
18	19	20	21	22	23	24
25	26	27	28	29	30	

3. 几 号?
Jǐ hào?

二十七 号
Èrshíqī hào.

4. 星期 几?
Xīngqī jǐ?

星期三。
Xīngqīsān.

几月大，几月小?

(Jǐ yuè dà, jǐ yuè xiǎo?)

Chinese children remember how many days there are in each month by memorising this chant. *Dà* (大) means that it is a 'big' month of 31 days, *xiǎo* (小) means that it is a 'small' month of 30 days or in the case of February, 28 days (or 29 days in a leap year).

一月大，二月小，
三月大，四月小，
五月大，六月小，
七月大，八月大，
九月小，十月大，
十一月小，
十二月大。

今天是星期几？ (Jīntiān shì xīngqī jǐ?)

今天 是……

Jīntiān 。 ...

星期一	星期二	星期三	星期四
xīngqīyī	xīngqī'èr	xīngqīsān	xīngqīsì
星期五	星期六	星期天	
xīngqīwǔ	xīngqīliù	xīngqītiān	

练一练 (Liàn yí liàn) →

Day, month and year

Here is how you express a date which includes the *day*, *month and year*.

一九八六年 六月 二十五 号

Yī jiǔ bā liù **nián** liù**yuè** èrshíwǔ **hào.**

If you wish to express the *date* and the *day of the week*, the sequence is:

一月 四号 星期六

yī**yuè** sì **hào** **xīngqī**liù

or, with the *year*:

一九九二年 一月 四号 星期六

Yī jiǔ jiǔ èr **nián** yī**yuè** sì **hào** **xīngqī**liù

How would you express the same date in English? Find all the differences between the Chinese and the English ways of saying these dates.

练一练 (Liàn yí liàn)

1. How would you express these years in Chinese?

   1207 1964
   1658 2000
   1901 2035

2. What do you think the months of January, July, October and December would be in Chinese?
3. How would you say these dates?

   2nd, 4th, 10th, 16th,
   22nd, 24th, 31st

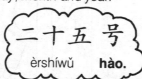

哪天？ (Něi tiān?)

昨天 今天 明天 后天

zuótiān jīntiān míngtiān hòutiān

今天 是 星期五。

Jīntiān 。 xīngqī 。

昨天 是 星期 几？

Zuótiān 。 xīngqī 。?

明天 是 星期 几？

Míngtiān 。 xīngqī 。?

后天 是 星期 几？

Hòutiān 。 xīngqī 。?

哪个星期？ (Něige xīngqī?)

上 个 星期

shàng gè xīngqī

这个 星期

zhèige xīngqī

下 个 星期

xià gè xīngqī

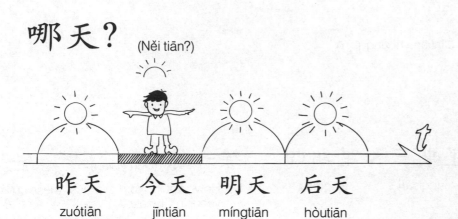

SUN MON TUE
1 2
7 8 9
14 15 16
21 22 23
28 29 30

这个 星期二 是 十七 号。

◦ ◦ xīngqī ◦ ◦ ◦ ◦ hào.

上 个 星期六 是 几 号？

◦ ◦ xīngqī ◦ ◦ ◦ hào?

下 个 星期一 是 几 号？

Xià ◦ xīngqī ◦ ◦ ◦ hào?

哪个月？ (Něige yuè?)

上 个 月	这个 月	下 个 月
shàng gè yuè	zhèi ge yuè	xià gè yuè
九月？	？	？

哪年？ (Něi nián?)

去年	今年	明年
qùnián	jīnnián	míngnián
？	？	1998

Nǐ tīngdǒng le ma? →

你听懂了吗？

(Nǐ tīngdǒng le ma?)

Which is true?

1. a) The boy told the girl they were having Chinese today.
   b) The boy did not know whether there was a Chinese lesson today.
   c) The boy said that there was no Chinese lesson today.
2. They have Chinese lessons on
   a) Thursdays
   b) Wednesdays
   c) Tuesdays

再见！

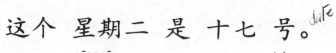

Here are some more phrases you often hear when people are saying goodbye.

Míngtiān (or *míngr*) *jiàn!* (明天/明儿见!)
Hòutiān jiàn (后天见!)
Xīngqīliù jiàn! (星期六见!)

When are they expecting to see each other next?

LEARN TO READ page 102

3.6 Today is my birthday

今天是你的生日吗?

(Jīntiān shì nǐ de shēngrì ma?)

林 兰兰: 今天 是 几 号?
∘ Lánlán:

李 国华: 今天 是……, 我 不 知道。
Lǐ ∘ huá

林 兰兰: 张 云, 你 知道 今天
∘ Lánlán: Zhāng Yún, ∘ ∘ ∘ ∘ ∘

是 几 号 吗?

张 云: 星期天 是 八 号,
Zhāng Yún:

今天 是 星期三……

九、十、十一……

今天 是 十一 号。

林 兰兰： 十一号？
∘ Lánlán:

那 今天 是 李 明 的 生日。
∘ ∘ ∘ ∘ Lǐ Míng ∘ ∘ rì.

张 云： 是 吗？
Zhāng Yún:

李 国华： 我 问问 他。……
Lǐ ∘ huá:

李 明，今天 是 你 的 生日
Lǐ Míng, ∘ ∘ ∘ ∘ ∘ ∘ rì

吗？
∘ ?

李 明： 是。
Lǐ Míng:

李 国华： 祝 你 生日 快乐！
Lǐ ∘ huá: Zhù ∘ ∘ ∘ kuàilè!

林 兰兰： 祝 你 生日 快乐！
∘ Lánlán: Zhù ∘ ∘ ∘ kuàilè!

张 云： 祝 你 生日 快乐！
Zhāng Yún: Zhù ∘ ∘ ∘ kuàilè!

李 明： 谢谢 大家！
Lǐ Míng:

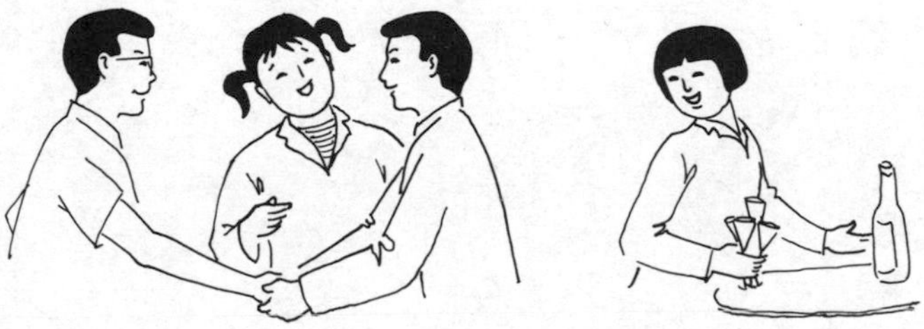

Note:
Nà jīntiān shì Lǐ Míng de shēngrì – *Nà* (那) here means ‘in that case’.

你的生日是几月几号?

Find the Chinese →
该你了!**(Gāi nǐ le!)** →

Find the Chinese

Then today is Li Ming's birthday.
Happy Birthday!
Thank you everybody!
Is it?
I'll ask him.

唱一唱 (Chàng yí chàng)

Now you can sing 'Happy Birthday' in Chinese:

祝你生日快乐!
祝你生日快乐!
祝你生日快乐!
祝你生日快乐!

该你了!(Gāi nǐ le!)

Is there a member of your family or a friend of yours who is about to have a birthday? Surprise them by designing a birthday card for them *in Chinese*! You can write on the card the date, who it is to, who it is from and the message 'Happy Birthday', all in Chinese. Use as many Chinese characters as you can but you can also use *pinyin*.

说汉语二 (Shuō Hànyǔ 2)

1. 老师: 今天 是 几 月 几 号?

阿伦: 今天 是 十 月 十九 号。
Ālún:

老师: 阿伦, 你 写在 黑板 上。
。 。: Ālún, 。 xiězài hēibǎn 。.

阿伦: 老师, 您 知道 吗?
Ālún: 。 。, nín 。 。 。?

今天 是 玛丽 的 生日。
。 。 。 Mǎlì 。 。 rì.

老师： 是吗？

玛丽，祝 你 生日 快乐！
Mǎlì, zhù 。 。 。 kuàilè!

2. 安娜： 阿伦，明天 是 你 的 生日 吧？
Ānnà: Ālún, míng 。 。 。 。 。 。 ba?

阿伦： 不 是，我 的 生日 是 二十三 号。
Ālún:

安娜： 哦，那 你 的 生日 是 下 个 星期一！
Ānnà: Ò, 。 。 。 。 rì 。 xià 。 。 。 。!

阿伦： 是。
Ālún:

Note:
Ālún, míngtiān shì nǐ de shēngrì ba? – *Ba* (吧) at the end of a statement indicates that the speaker is asking for confirmation. In this case, Anna is not sure whether the next day was in fact Alan's birthday. More examples:

Tā shì Lǐ lǎoshī ba?
Jīntiān shì xīngqīsān ba?
Zhèi zhī bǐ shì Mǎlì de ba?

Find the Chinese →

LEARN TO READ page 103

LEARN TO WRITE Lesson 10 page 112

Find the Chinese

Happy birthday, Mary!
Please write it on the blackboard.
No, my birthday's on the 23rd.
It's your birthday tomorrow, isn't it?
Next Monday.

学会认字 (Xuéhuì rèn zì)

3.1

Before reading the text, listen to the recording and answer the questions.

True or false?
1. The woman has heard that the 40th Middle School is a large school.
2. The boy thinks it is not a large school at all.
3. He does not know how many students there are.

汉字表 (Hànzì biǎo)

			As in
哪	něi	*which*	哪个中学?
校	xiào	*school*	学校
很	hěn	*very*	很大
多	duō	*many*	多少?
少	shǎo	*few*	
知	zhī	*to know*	知道
道	dào	*way*	

Text

W: 你上哪个中学?
B: 四十中。
W: 四十中?
你们的学校很大，是吗?
B: 是，我们的学校很大。
W: 你们的学校有多少个学生?
B: 我不知道。

动动脑筋!

(Dòngdong nǎojīn!)

See if you can guess what these words might mean or work out the answers to the questions.

1. 多多少少
   a) more or less
   b) a lot or a little
2. Give two examples of a
   校名
3. 住校
   Who do you think would be most likely to do this?
   a) a doctor
   b) a student
   c) a bus driver
4. A 多国 company is a … company?

3.2

Before reading the text, listen to the recording and answer the questions.

True or false?
1. The owner of the pen was unknown to the first student.
2. Wang Li is known to the girl.
3. Wang Li did not want the pen.

汉字表 (Hànzì biǎo)

			As in
笔	bǐ	*writing implement*	
问	wèn	*to ask*	请问
给	gěi	*to give*	给你
谢	xiè	*to thank*	谢谢

Text

G: 这是谁的笔？
A: 我看看，……不是我的。

G: 请问，这是谁的笔？
B: 是王利的。

G: 王利，这是你的笔吗？
C: 是我的。

G: 给你。
C: 谢谢你。
G: 不谢。

3.3

Before reading the text, listen to the recording and answer the questions.

Dialogue 1:
True or false?
1. The student wanted to know the word for 'this'.
2. The student wanted to know the word for 'textbook'.

Dialogue 2:
True of false?
1. The boy told the girl to ask Teacher Xie the question.
2. The girl said he was a good boy.
3. The girl was not sure that she had pronounced the word correctly.
4. The teacher was very pleased.

汉字表 (Hànzì biǎo)

			As in
文	wén	*script; writing; language*	中文
怎	zěn	*how*	怎么
说	shuō	*to say, speak*	
课	kè	*lesson*	上课
本	běn	*(measure word)*	课本
懂	dǒng	*to understand*	懂了

Text

1. A: 老师，这个中文怎么说?
   B: 这个中文叫"课本"。
   懂了吗?
   A: 懂了。

2. G: 请问，"Australia" 中文怎么说?
   B: 我不知道，你问问谢老师。
   G: 好。
   ……

G: 谢老师，请问，"Australia" 中文怎么说？

X: "Australia" 中文叫"澳大利亚"。

G: "澳–大–利–亚"，对吗？

X: 对了！很好！

3.4

Before reading the text, listen to the recording and answer the questions.

True or false?

1. A *xiǎoshuō* is a kind of writing instrument.
2. The boy wanted to borrow one.
3. The boy had to make a choice.
4. The girl felt he had made the right choice.

汉字表 (Hànzì biǎo)

			As in
借	jiè	*to lend; borrow*	借给我
要	yào	*to want*	你要哪本？
可	kě	(*as in* kě hǎokàn le)	

Text

B: 这两本小说是你的还是她的？

G: 是我的。

B: 借给我一本，好吗？

G: 好，你要哪本？

B: 我要这本。

G: 那本可好看了。

3.5

Before reading the text, listen to the recording and answer the questions.

Dialogue 1:
True or false?
1. The boy thought today was the 7th.
2. The girl said it was the 16th.
3. It was a Thursday.

Dialogue 2:
True or false?
1. The boy thought that Wednesday was the 16th.
2. The girl said the 16th was Monday.
3. The boy was wrong.

汉字表 (Hànzì biǎo)

			As in
今	jīn	*present*	今天
天	tiān	*day; sky*	
号	hào	*number; date*	几号？
星	xīng	*star*	星期
期	qī	*period of time*	
月	yuè	*month; moon*	三月
年	nián	*year*	今年

Text

1. B: 今天几号？
   G: 今天十六号。
   B: 星期几？
   G: 星期四。

2. B: 星期三是十六号吗？
G: 今天是星期一，……十四号。
十四，十五，十六，
星期三是十六号。
B: 谢谢。
G: 不谢。

3. Q: 今天是几月几号？
A: 今天是一九九八年
七月二十五号。

动动脑筋！

(Dòngdong nǎojīn!)

See if you can guess what these words might mean. They are made up of characters you know.

老年
老年人

3.6

Before reading the text, listen to the recording and answer the questions.

Dialogue 1
True or false?
1. The girl was asking what day Xiao Ming's birthday was.
2. The boy and Xiao Ming share the same birthday.
3. Xiao Ming's birthday is on 26 May.
4. The girl has her birthday after the boy's.

Dialogue 2:
1. Today is the girl's birthday.
2. The girl did not believe the boy.

汉字表 (Hànzì biǎo)

			As in
明	míng	*bright, clear*	明天
日	rì	*day; sun*	生日
下	xià	*next; to leave*	下个星期
祝	zhù	*to express good wishes*	祝你……
快	kuài	*happy; soon; quick*	快乐
乐	lè	*happy*	

Text

1. G: 今天几号？
   B: 二十五号。
   G: 今天二十五号？
   那明天是小明的生日！
   B: 是吗？
   我的生日也是五月二十六号！
   你的生日呢？
   G: 我的生日是六月三号，
   B: 那是……下个星期六。
   G: 是。

2. B: 今天是我的生日。
   G: 是吗？今天也是我的生日！
   B: 祝你生日快乐！
   G: 祝你生日快乐！

动动脑筋！

(Dòngdong nǎojīn!)

See if you can guess what these words might mean or work out the answers to the questions.

1. If someone is said to be
   七上八下
   it means that that person is
   a) perturbed or agitated
   b) about seven or eight years old
   c) moving up and down
2. If someone is described as being
   三十岁上下
   how old do you think he or she would be?
3. 天下一家
4. Which of these things is expected to
   上天？
   a) a skyscraper
   b) a cable car
   c) a spacecraft
5. Which branch of learning do you think
   天文
   refers to?

Summary

3.1 Our classroom

Now you can:

identify places, objects and people:
Zhè shì wǒmen de jiàoshì. 这是我们的教室。
Zhè shì wǒ de shūbāo. 这是我的书包。
Nà shì Wáng Huá. 那是王华。
Huáng lǎoshī shì wǒmen de Yīngyǔ lǎoshī. 黄老师是我们的英语老师。

3.2 Whose is it?

Now you can:

ask about ownership:
Zhè shì nǐ de bǐ ma? 这是你的笔吗？
Nǐ zhīdao shì shéi de ma? 你知道是谁的吗？

say you picked something up:
Wǒ jiǎndào yì zhī bǐ. 我捡到一支笔。

say you thought something was lost:
Wǒ yǐwéi tā diū le ne! 我以为它丢了呢！

respond politely to someone's thanks:
Bú xiè. 不谢。
Búyòng kèqi. 不用客气。

Useful expressions
Wǒ kànkan ... （我看看……） *Let me have a look ...*

Grammar and usage reference
Repetition of verb page 81
Diū le （丢了） page 81
Courteous responses to Xièxie（谢谢）。 page 81

3.3 How do you say it?

Now you can:

ask how to say something in another language:
"Dìtú" Yīngwén jiào shénme? "地图"英文叫什么？
"Map of China" Zhōngwén zěnme shuō? "Map of China" 中文怎么说？

ask if something has been understood:
Dàjiā dǒng le ma? 大家懂了吗？

announce the beginning or end of class:
Shàngkè le! 上课了！
Xiàkè! 下课！

ask for something to be repeated:
Qǐng nǐ zài shuō yí biàn. 请你再说一遍。

Useful expressions
Dǒng le. 懂了。*I understand.*
Bú duì. 不对。*That's wrong.*

Usage reference
Hànyǔ (汉语), *Zhōngguóhuà* (中国话) and Zhōngwén (中文) page 83
Classroom routine page 84

3.4 Which one is it?

Now you can:

ask which one:
Nèi gè qiú shí nǐ de háishi tā de? 那个球是你的还是他的？
"Kèběn" Yīngwén shì *"exercise book"* háishi *"textbook"*? "课本"英文是 *"exercise book"* 还是 *"textbook"*?
Nǐ yào něige? 你要哪个？

ask if you can borrow a book:
Jiè(gěi) wǒ kànkan, hǎo ma? 借(给)我看看，好吗？
Jiè(gěi) wǒ yì běn, hǎo ma? 借(给)我一本，好吗？

say which one of something you want:
Wǒ yào zhèige. 我要这个。
Wǒ yào zhèi běn (shū). 我要这本(书)。

Useful expressions

..., hǎo ma? (……好吗?) *Could I ...?/How about ...? (making a request or a suggestion)*

Grammar and usage reference

Xiē (些) page 86
Omission of noun following measure word page 86
Measure word list page 87
Zhèi (这), *nèi* (那), *něi* (哪) page 89

3.5 What is the date today?

Now you can:

ask what the date is:

Jīntiān shì jǐ yuè jǐ hào? 今天是几月几号？

express dates:

Yī jiǔ bā liù nián liùyuè èrshíwǔ hào. 一九八六年六月二十五号。
Yīyuè sì hào xīngqīliù. 一月四号星期六。

say goodbye by saying when you will meet again:

Míngtiān jiàn! 明天见！
Míngnián jiàn! 明年见！
Xīngqīliù jiàn! 星期六见！
Xià gè xīngqī jiàn! 下个星期见！

Grammar and usage reference

Sequence when expressing dates page 91
Saying 'Goodbye' page 94

3.6 Today is my birthday

Now you can:

wish someone 'Happy Birthday!':

Zhù nǐ shēngrì kuàilè! 祝你生日快乐！

ask for confirmation of a fact you are uncertain of:

Ālún, míngtiān shì nǐ de shēngrì ba? 阿伦，明天是你的生日吧？

ask someone to write something on the blackboard:

Qǐng nǐ xiězài hēibǎn shàng. 请你写在黑板上。

Useful expressions
Nà ... (那……) *Then ....*
Shì ma? (是吗?) Is that so?

Grammar and usage reference
Nà (那) meaning 'in that case' page 95
Ba (吧) asking for confirmation page 97

学会写字 第八课 (Xuéhuì xiě zì Dì-bā kè)

汉字表 (Hànzì biǎo)

Basic stroke		
As in	么	哪

什	shén *as in* shénme	么	me *as in* shénme
名	míng *name*	字	zì *character; word; letters*
呢	ne *(sentence particle)*	哪	něi *which*

Text

A: 你叫什么名字?

B: 我叫……, 你呢?

A: 我叫……, 你上哪个中学?

B: 我上五十六中, 你呢?

A: 我上四十七中。

学会写字 第九课 (Xuéhuì xiě zì Dì-jiǔ kè)

汉字表 (Hànzì biǎo)

Basic stroke		
As in	很	谁

	ma *(question particle)*		hěn *very*

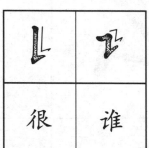

那	nà *that*	谁	shéi *who*
大	dà *big*	校	xiào *school*

Text

A: 你好吗？

B: 很好，你呢？

A: 我也很好……那是谁？

B: 那是我姐姐。

A: 她也是我们学校的学生吗？

B: 不是，她上大学。

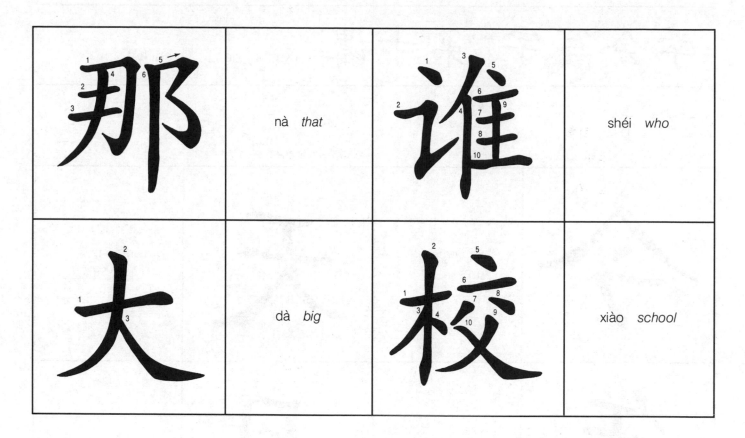

学会写字 第十课 (Xuéhuì xiě zì Dì-shí kè)

汉字表 (Hànzì biǎo)

今	jīn *present*	天	tiān *day; heaven*
年	nián *year*	月	yuè *month; moon*
号	hào *number; date*	星	xīng *star*

期	qī *period of time*	日	rì *day; sun*
下	xià *to leave; next*	明	míng *bright*

Text

a) 今天是一九九三年六月八号星期五。
今天是小明的生日。

b) 下个星期六九月二十七号
是我的生日。

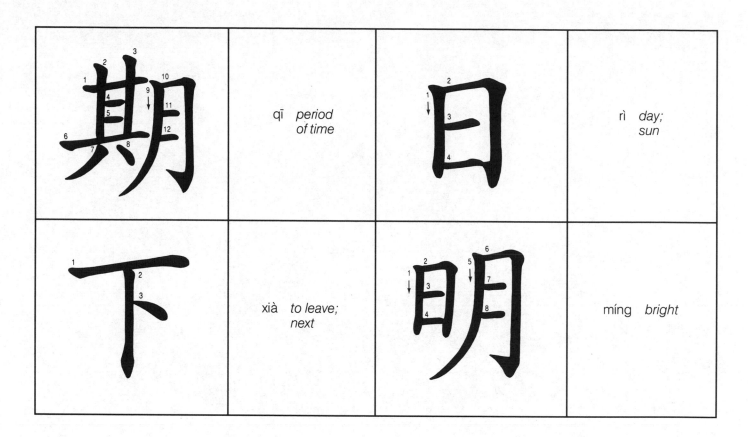

UNIT 4 Daily Routine

第四单元
Dì-sì dānyuán

我的一天
Wǒ de yì tiān

In this unit you will learn how to talk about the time, your daily routine and about travelling by various means of transport. You will also learn how to describe the weather.

4.1 What is the time?

现在几点？ (Xiànzài jǐ diǎn?)

To ask what time it is, you say:

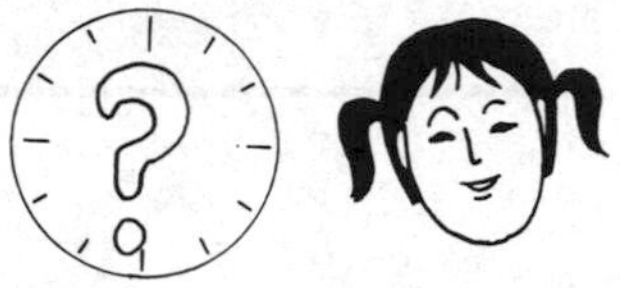

现在 几 点？

Xiànzài 。 diǎn?

When answering, you may say:

……点。

… diǎn

e.g. 

现在 十 点。

Xiànzài 。 diǎn.

or

现在……点

Xiànzài … diǎn.

八 点 零 五 分

。 diǎn líng 。 fēn.

八 点 十 分

。 diǎn 。 fēn

八 点 二十五 分

。 diǎn 。 。 。 fēn

八 点 一 刻

。 diǎn 。 kè

八 点 半

。 diǎn bàn

八 点 三 刻

。 diǎn 。 kè

a.m. and p.m.

To indicate whether it is a.m. or p.m., all you have to do is to mention the period during the day *before* the hour and/or minute, e.g.

早上	上午	中午	下午	晚上
zǎoshang	shàngwǔ	zhōngwǔ	xiàwǔ	wǎnshang

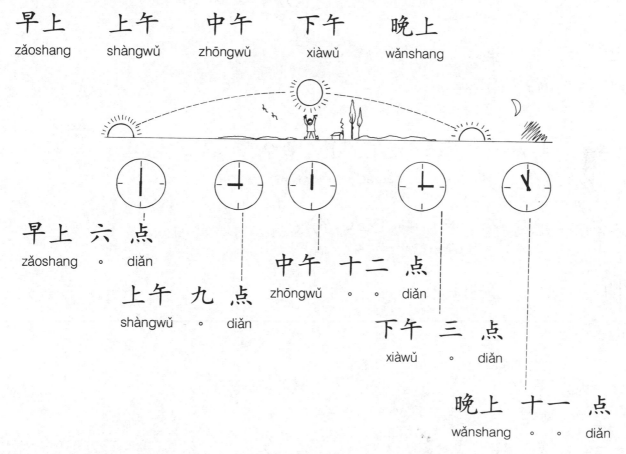

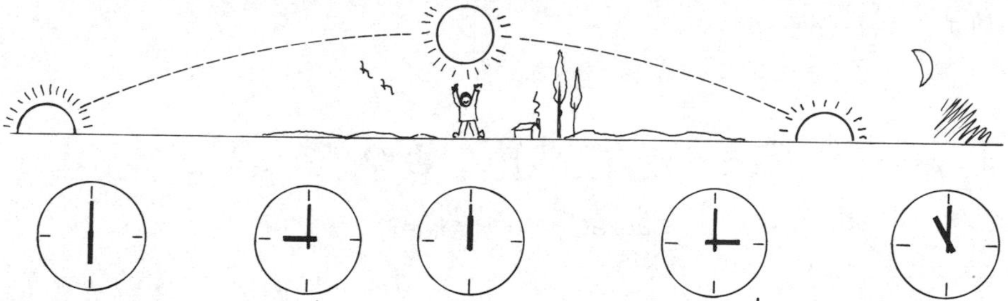

早上 六 点
zǎoshang ◦ diǎn

上午 九 点
shàngwǔ ◦ diǎn

中午 十二 点
zhōngwǔ ◦ ◦ diǎn

下午 三 点
xiàwǔ ◦ diǎn

晚上 十一 点
wǎnshang ◦ ◦ diǎn

Note:
Zǎoshang (早上) and *shàngwǔ* (上午) may both refer to the morning in a general way; for example, both these sentences refer to something happening 'tomorrow morning':

Nǐ míngtiān zǎoshang yǒu Hànyǔ kè ma?	Do you have Chinese lessons tomorrow morning?
Nǐ míngtiān shàngwǔ jiè(gěi) wǒ, hǎo ma?	Could you lend it to me tomorrow morning?

When used in indicating clock time, both *zǎoshang* or *shàngwǔ* are used. *Zǎoshang* roughly refers to the hours of the morning before, say, 9 o'clock; whereas *shàngwǔ* refers to the hours after 9 o'clock, e.g.

zǎoshang bā diǎn bàn 早上八点半
shàngwǔ shíyī diǎn 上午十一点

说汉语一 (Shuō Hànyǔ 1)

1. A: 安娜，现在 几 点？
Ānnà ◦ ◦ ◦ diǎn?

B: 现在 五 点 半。
Xiànzài ◦ diǎn bàn

2. A: 劳 驾，现在 几 点？
Láo jià, xiànzài ◦ diǎn?

B: 六 点 三十五 分。
◦ diǎn. ◦ ◦ ◦ fēn.

A: 谢谢。

3. A: 现在 几 点？
Xiànzài ◦ diǎn?

B: 对不起，我 不 知道。
Duìbuqǐ, ◦ ◦ ◦ ◦.

A: 劳 驾，现在 几 点？
Láo jià, xiànzài ◦ diǎn?

C: 九 点 半。
◦ diǎn bàn.

A: 哎哟，我 的 表 慢 了。
Āiyō, ◦ ◦ biǎo màn ◦.

咱们 晚 了！
Zán ◦ wǎn ◦!

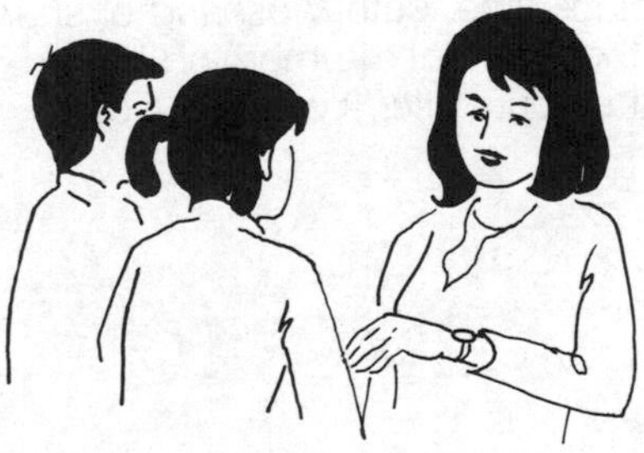

B: 那 咱们 快 走 吧!
∘ zán ∘ kuài zǒu ba!

A: 谢谢。

C: 不 客气。
∘ kèqi.

Note:
Zánmen wǎn le! – You have already learnt to say *wǒmen* (我们) meaning 'we' or 'us'. *Zánmen* (咱们) also means 'we' or 'us', but with an important difference.

When you say **zánmen** you are including the person or persons you are speaking to.

Zánmen zǒu ba!
Zhè shì zánmen de shū.

When you say ***wǒmen*** you may or may not be including the listener(s).

Wǒmen shì xuésheng.
Nǐmen shì Àodàlìyàrén ma?
Wǒmen shì Zhōngguórén.

Find the Chinese →
Nǐ tīngdǒng le ma? →

LEARN TO READ page 138

LEARN TO WRITE Lesson 11 page 148

Find the Chinese

Oh dear, my watch is slow.
Excuse me please ...
We'd better hurry then!
We're late!
Don't mention it. (*polite response*)

你听懂了吗?

(Nǐ tīngdǒng le ma?)

True or false?

a) The man's watch was about 10 minutes too slow.
b) The man's watch was indicating the correct time.
c) The man's watch was approximately 7 minutes too fast.

4.2 Daily routine

玲玲的一天 (Línglíng de yì tiān)

早上
zǎo 。

上午
。
before
shang. wǔ
(midday)

中午
。
zhong wǔ
midday

玲玲 早上 六 点 起床。
Línglíng zǎo 。 。 。 qǐchuáng.

她 七 点 半 去 上学。
。 。 。 。 qù 。 。

玲玲 上午 八 点 上课。
Línglíng 。 。 。 。 。 。

玲玲 上午 九 点 五十分
Línglíng 。 。 。 。 。 。

做 课间操。
zuò 。 jiāncāo. (exercise)

她 中午 十二 点 吃 午饭。
。 。 。 。 。 。 chī 。 fàn.
wǔ

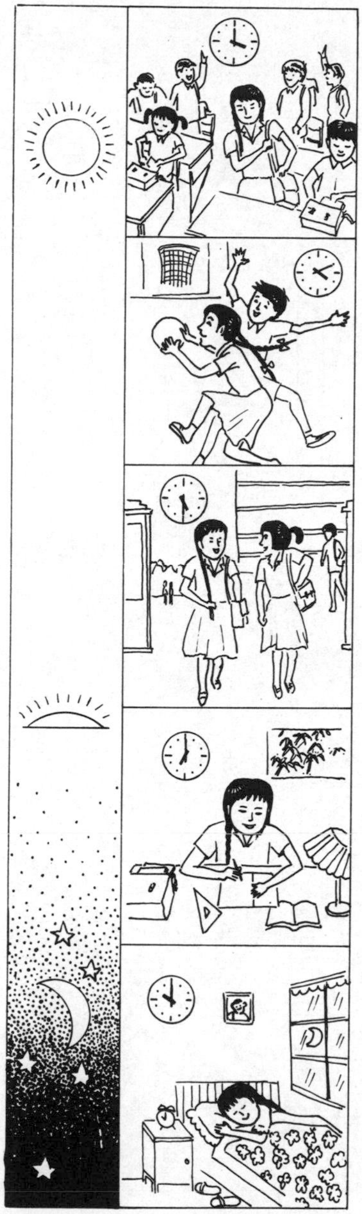

下午
next *wǔ*

她 下午 四 点 下课。

她 四 点 十 分 去 打球。
　　　　　　　qù　dǎ　qiú.

她 五 点 半 放学 回家。
　　　　　fàng　huí

她 晚上 七 点 做 作业。
　wǎn　　　　　zuò　zuòyè.

她 晚上 十 点
　wǎn

睡觉。
shuìjiào.
sleep

晚上
wǎn
shang
eve

fàng xue finish school
huí - return
jia - home

zuò - to
zuòyè - homework

该 你 了！ (Gāi nǐ le!)

Now you can say something about your own daily routine.

你 听懂 了 吗？

(Nǐ tīngdǒng le ma?)

1. Which is true?
 a) The boy wants to show Peter his pet dog.
 b) He wants to see Peter's pet dog.
 c) He wants Peter to see the girl's pet dog.
2. True or false?
 a) The girl finishes at different times during the week.
 b) She finishes at 4 o'clock every day of the week.
 c) She finishes at 4.30 every day of the week.

Note:
Chī wǔfàn (吃午饭) means 'have lunch'. What do you think the following phrases mean?

吃 晚饭　　　　吃 早饭
chī　wǎnfàn　　chī　zǎofàn
　　　　　　　eat *breakfast*

该 你 了！(Gāi nǐ le!) →
Nǐ tīngdǒng le ma? →

chī eat

说汉语二 (Shuō Hànyǔ 2)

1. A: 你 每 天 早上 几 点 起床？
◦ měi ◦ zǎo ◦ ◦ ◦ qǐchuáng?

B: 七 点 半，你 呢？

A: 我 七 点 十五 分 起床。
◦ ◦ ◦ ◦ ◦ ◦ qǐchuáng.

2. A: 你 每 天 晚上 做 什么？
◦ měi ◦ wǎn ◦ zuò ◦ ◦?

B: 我 有 时候 看 书，
◦ ◦ shíhou ◦ shū,

有 时候 看 电视，你 呢？
◦ shíhou ◦ diànshì, ◦ ◦?

A: 我 六 点 吃 晚饭，
◦ ◦ ◦ chī wǎnfàn,

然后 做 作业，
ránhòu zuò zuòyè,

有 时候 还 看看 电视。
◦ shíhou ◦ ◦ ◦ diànshì.

Find the Chinese →

LEARN TO READ page 139

LEARN TO WRITE Lesson 12 page 149

Find the Chinese

Sometimes I read.
I have dinner at 6.00.
Sometimes I also watch TV.
After that I do my homework.
What do you do each evening?

4.3 Shall we go by bus?

坐什么车? (Zuò shénme chē?)

坐
zuò

坐 汽车
zuò qìchē

坐 公共 汽车
zuò gōnggòng qìchē

坐 电车
zuò diànchē

坐 火车
zuò huǒchē

骑
qí

骑 自行车
qí zìxíngchē

骑 摩托车
qí mótuōchē

骑 马
qí mǎ

走
zǒu

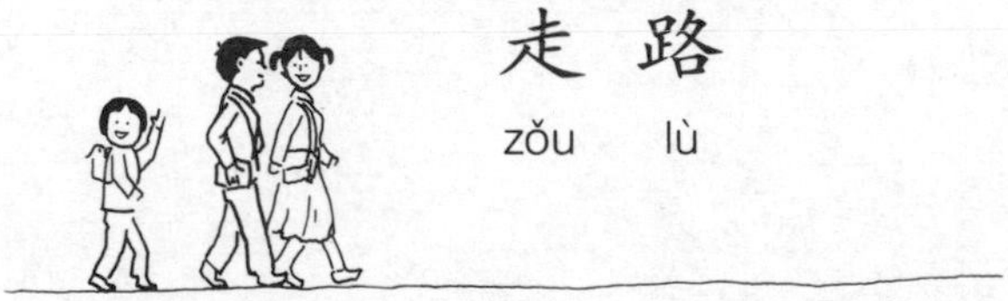

走 路
zǒu lù

qù - go
qí - Travel

Notes:

1. *Chē* (车) means 'vehicle'. Hence, it forms part of many words for vehicles of different kinds, e.g.

   zìxíngchē bicycle
   qìchē car
   gōnggòng qìchē bus
   diànchē tram
   wúguǐ diànchē trolley bus
   mǎchē horse-drawn cart
   huǒchē train
   kǎchē truck
   mótuōchē motorcycle
   miànbāochē mini-bus
   chūzū qìchē taxi

2. Privately owned cars are very rare in China, and people tend to use public transport much more than we do. Therefore, when someone says *zuò chē* (坐车), he or she would generally be referring to travelling by bus (or trolley-bus), which is a very common form of public transport.
   Most families own a bike or two, or even a motorbike or scooter. The *chē* in *qí chē* (骑车) could refer to any of these vehicles.

他怎么上学? (Tā zěnme shàngxué?)

Pictures:

1. A: 李 云 怎么 上学?
   Lǐ Yún ◦ ◦ ◦ ◦?

   B: 李 云 骑 车 上学。
   Lǐ Yún qí chē ◦ ◦.

2. A: 张 建 的 爸爸 怎么 上班?
   Zhāng Jiàn ◦ ◦ ◦ ◦ ◦ bān?

   B: 张 建 的 爸爸
   Zhāng Jiàn ◦ ◦ ◦

   坐 公共 汽车 上班。
   zuò gōnggòng qìchē ◦ bān.

3. A: 他们 怎么 回 家?

B: 他们 坐 电车 回 家。

◦ ◦ zuò diànchē ◦ ◦.

4. A: 玲玲 怎么 去 学校?

Línglíng ◦ ◦ qù ◦ ◦?

B: 她 每天 走 路 去 学校。

◦ ◦ ◦ zǒu lù qù ◦ ◦

Tā	**zěnme**	huí jiā? shàngxué shàngbān qù xuéxiào
Tā	**qí** zìxíngchē **zuò** qìchē zuò gōnggòng qìchē zuò huǒchē **zǒu lù**	huí jiā. shàngxué shàngbān qù xuéxiào

咱们快走吧! (Zánmen kuài zǒu ba!)

林 方: 快 一点儿, 好 吗?

◦ ◦: ◦ yìdiǎnr, ◦ ◦?

李 云: 着 什么 急 呢?

Lǐ Yún: Zháo ◦ ◦ jí ◦?

现在 几 点?

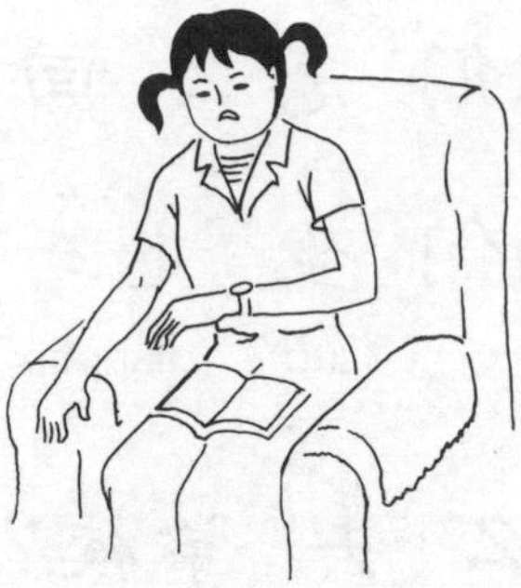

林 方： 快 五 点 了！

李 云： 哎哟，我 的 表 慢 了！
Lǐ Yún: Āiyō, ° ° biǎo màn °!

你 的 自行车 呢？
° ° zìxíngchē °?

林 方： 骑 车 太 慢 了。
° ° Qí chē tài màn °.

咱们 坐 公共 汽车 吧！
Zán ° zuò gōnggòng qìchē ba!

李 云： 好。
Lǐ Yún:

林 方： 那 咱们 快 走 吧！
° °: ° zán ° kuài zǒu ba!

Note:
Qí chē tài màn le! – *Tài* ... (太....) means 'too ...' indicating an excess of something. Sentences where *tài* ... is used often end with *le* (了), e.g.
Zhèi zhāng zhuōzi tài dà le. 这张桌子太大了。

In the opinion of the speaker, what is wrong with the table?

Find the Chinese →
Nǐ tīngdǒng le ma? →

LEARN TO READ page 140

LEARN TO WRITE Lesson 13 page 150

Find the Chinese

Let's hurry up and go then!
It's nearly 5.00!
Could you hurry up a bit?
Where's your bike?
What's the rush?
Let's go by bus!
Bikes are too slow.

你听懂了吗？

(Nǐ tīngdǒng le ma?)

Which of these statements are true?

1. a) The girl usually goes home by bike.
   b) She usually takes the bus home.
   c) She never rides a bike home.
2. a) The girl was unable to borrow her mother's bike today.
   b) She borrowed her mother's bike to go to work today.
   c) Her mother borrowed her bike to go somewhere.

4.4 What are they doing?

他们正在做什么？

(Tāmen zhèngzài zuò shénme?)

现在 九 点 了。

同学们 正在 等 老师。

∘ ∘ ∘ zhèng ∘ děng ∘ ∘.

他们 正在 做 什么？

∘ ∘ zhèng ∘ ∘ ∘ ∘?

王 云 正在 画 画儿。

∘ Yún zhèng ∘ huà huàr.

他 的 画儿 真 好看！

∘ ∘ huàr ∘ ∘ ∘!

刘 新 正在 听 音乐。

Liú Xīn zhèng ∘ tīng yīnyuè.

他 正在 听 摇滚乐。

∘ zhèng ∘ tīng yáogǔnyuè.

刘 方 正在 写 信。

Liú ∘ zhèng ∘ xiě xìn.

她 的 朋友 很 多。

∘ ∘ péngyou ∘ ∘.

张建很着急。

Zhāng Jiàn ∘ zháojí.

他正在赶作业。

∘ zhèng ∘ gǎn ∘ ∘.

王书正在打球。

∘ Shū zhēng ∘ dǎ qiú.

他是球迷。

∘ ∘ qiúmí.

白云正在吃东西。

Bái Yún zhèng ∘ ∘ dōngxi.

她饿了。

∘ è ∘.

八点了，李明正在做什么呢?

∘ ∘ ∘, Lǐ ∘ zhèng ∘ ∘ ∘ ∘ ∘?

他正在睡觉。他累了。

∘ zhèng ∘ ∘ ∘. ∘ lèi ∘.

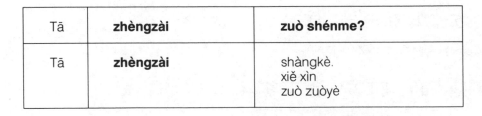

Note:
Xiànzài jiǔ diǎn le. — *Le* (了) indicates a change in the situation, i.e. that it is now 9.00. The answer to the question *Xiànzài jǐ diǎn?* may be either *Xiànzài … diǎn* or *Xiànzài … diǎn le.*

Tā	**zhèngzài**	**zuò shénme?**
Tā	**zhèngzài**	shàngkè. xiě xìn zuò zuòyè

你们正在做什么?

Note:
This is how you reply to a question such as *Tā **zhèngzài** huà huàr ma?*

	Tā	zhèngzài	kàn shū	ma?
Shì,	tā	zhèngzài	kàn shū.	
Méiyǒu,	tā	méiyǒu	kàn shū.	

If you know that the person is doing something else (e.g. listening to music) and wish to say so, you may answer:

***Méiyǒu**, tā zhèngzài tīng yīnyuè.*

练一练 (Liàn yí liàn) →

练一练 (Liàn yí liàn)

大卫正在睡觉吗?

说汉语三 (Shuō Hànyǔ 3)

(The phone rings at Lingling's home.)

玲玲： 喂，你 找 谁？
Língling: Wèi, ◦ zhǎo ◦?

小明： 哦，玲玲，我 是 小明！
Ò, Língling, ◦ ◦ ◦ ◦!

玲玲： 哦，小明，你 好！
Língling: Ò, ◦ ◦, ◦ ◦!

小明： 你好！

喂，你 正在 做 什么？
Wèi, ◦ zhèng ◦ ◦ ◦ ◦?

玲玲： 我 正在 赶 作业，你 呢？
Língling: ◦ zhèng ◦ gǎn ◦ ◦, ◦ ◦?

小明： 我 没有 作业，

我 正在 听 音乐。
◦ zhèng ◦ tīng yīnyuè.

下午 咱们 去 打 球，好 吗？
◦ ◦ zán ◦ qù dǎ qiú, ◦ ◦?

玲玲： 几 点？
Língling:

小明： 四 点 半。

玲玲： 现在 几 点，你 知道 吗？
Língling:

Find the Chinese

See you soon!
How about playing tennis this afternoon?
Hello, who would you like to speak to?
All right, I'll go by bike too.
I'm catching up on my homework.
All right then, we'll go at 4.30.

小明： 十二 点 二十 分。

玲玲： 那 好，咱们 四 点 半 去。
Línglíng: 。 。， zán 。 。 。 。 qù.

你 怎么 去 呢？

小明： 我 骑 车 去。
。 qí chē qù.

玲玲： 好，我 也 骑 车 去。
Línglíng: 。， 。 。 qí chē qù.

小明： 那 一会儿 见！
。 yíhuìr 。!

玲玲： 一会儿 见！
Línglíng: Yíhuìr 。!

Notes:

1. *Xiǎo Míng, nǐ hǎo!* – Lingling is addressing Xiao Ming by his childhood name. When used this way *xiǎo* (小) precedes one's given name, not the surname. Note that when the given name is made up of two characters (e.g. Jianhua), *xiǎo* precedes either one of the two characters, not both (i.e. either Xiao Jian *or* Xiao Hua).

2. *Wèi* (喂) is used to attract someone's attention, as in the sentence *Wèi, xiàwǔ zánmen qù dǎ qiú, hǎo ma?* It is also used when starting off a telephone conversation, much as you would say 'Hello'.

Find the Chinese page 130
Nǐ tīngdǒng le ma? →
该你了！**(Gāi nǐ le!)** →

LEARN TO READ page 141

你听懂了吗？

(Nǐ tīngdǒng le ma?)

1. Which is true?
   a) i) She knew it was David who answered the phone.
   ii) Anna thought it was David who answered the phone.
   iii) She thought it was David's father who answered the phone.
   b) i) Anna and David arranged to meet each other.
   ii) David did not want to go to Anna's place.
2. Which is true?
   a) i) The boy was doing his homework as well as watching TV.
   ii) He was not watching TV.
   iii) He was not doing his homework.
   b) His father went to bed early because
   i) He was too tired to catch the train.
   ii) He gets up at 5 every day to catch the train.
   iii) He has to get up at 5 the following morning to catch the train.

该你了！ (Gāi nǐ le!)

Make an arrangement with someone about doing some activity, e.g.
zhǎo péngyou (see friends)
qù dǎ qiú
qù tīng yīnyuè
You could suggest an activity (e.g. *Zánmen …, hǎo ma?*), then arrange with your partner what time to go and how to get there. When you say goodbye to each other, you can confirm the meeting time, (e.g. *Nà sān diǎn bàn jiàn!*).

4.5 What's the weather like?

今天天气挺好的！
(Jīntiān tiānqì tǐng hǎo de!)

今天 天气 很 热。
∘ ∘ ∘ qì ∘ rè.

今天 天气 很 冷。
∘ ∘ ∘ qì ∘ lěng.

现在 刮 风。
∘ ∘ guā fēng.

现在 下 雨。
∘ ∘ ∘ yǔ.

天气怎么样？ (Tiānqì zěnmeyàng?)

1. A: 天气 怎么样？
∘ qì ∘ ∘ yàng?

B: 天气 很 热。
∘ qì ∘ rè.

2. A: 今天 天气 怎么样?
◦ ◦ ◦ qì ◦ ◦ yàng?

B: 今天 天气 很 冷。
◦ ◦ ◦ qì ◦ lěng.

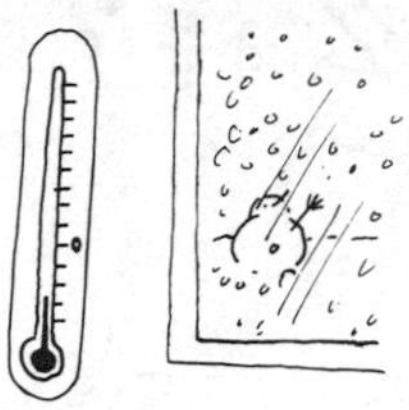

3. A: 现在 天气 怎么样?
◦ ◦ ◦ qì ◦ ◦ yàng?

B: 现在 正在 刮 风, 下 雨。
◦ ◦ ◦ ◦ guā fēng, ◦ yǔ.

4. A: 现在 天气 怎么样?
◦ ◦ ◦ qì ◦ ◦ yàng?

B: 现在 天气 挺 好 的;
◦ ◦ ◦ qì ◦ ◦ ◦.

不 冷, 也 不 热。
◦ lěng, ◦ ◦ rè.

A: 那 咱们 去 打 球 吧!
◦ zán ◦ qù dǎ qiú ba!

B: 走!

Find the Chinese →

Find the Chinese

Neither hot nor cold.
Let's go!
Just now it's windy and it's raining.
Let's go and have a game (*e.g. of tennis*) then!
It's very cold today.

北京今天天气怎么样?

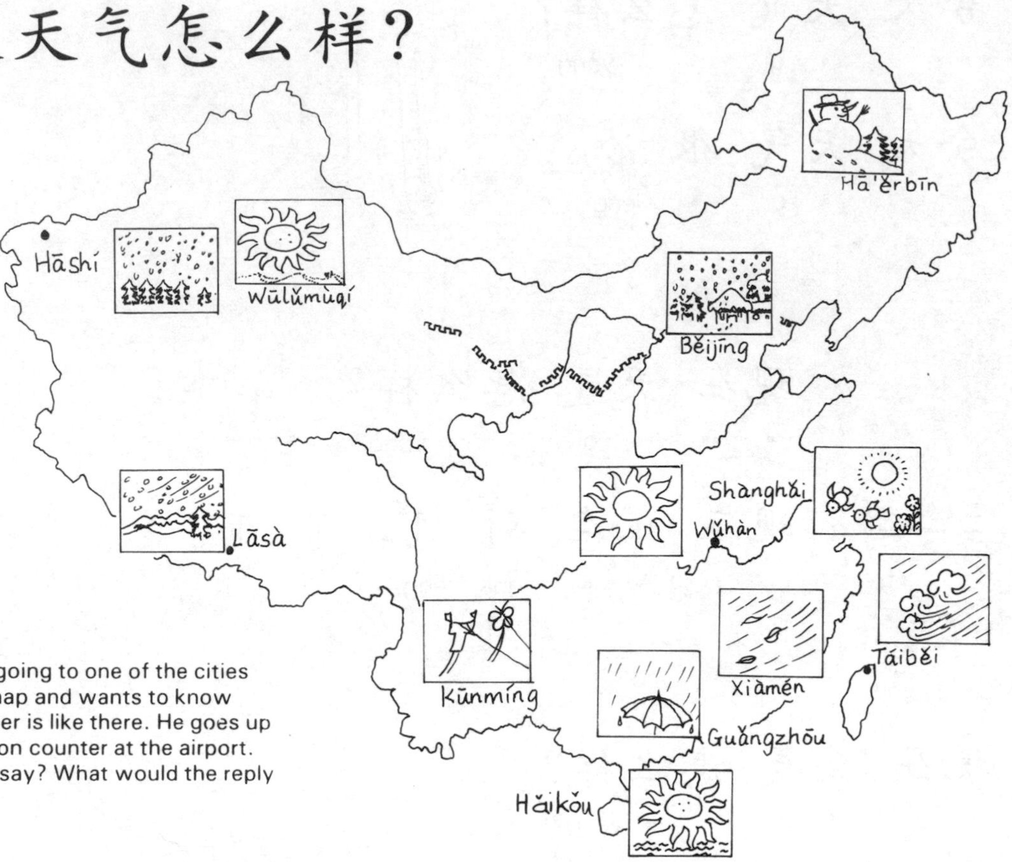

A traveller is going to one of the cities shown on the map and wants to know what the weather is like there. He goes up to the information counter at the airport. What would he say? What would the reply be?

我不怕!

Wǒ bú pà!

我不怕热！ (Wǒ bú pà rè!)

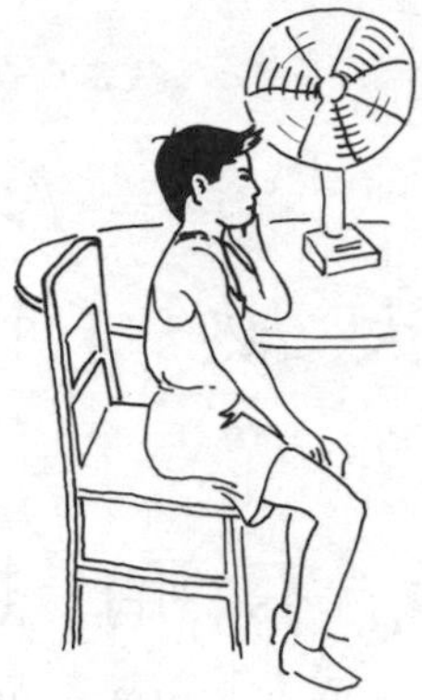

小明： 真 是 无聊！
∘ ∘ wúliáo!

大雷： 是 啊，没 事儿 干！
∘ Léi: ∘ a, ∘ shìr gàn!

小明： 咱们 去 打 球 吧！
Zán ∘ qù dǎ qiú ba!

大雷： 我 不 去，今天 天气 太 热 了，
∘ Léi: ∘ ∘ qù, ∘ ∘ ∘ qì tài rè ∘

我 怕 热。
∘ pà rè.

妈妈： 喂，你们 没有 事儿，
Wèi, ∘ ∘ ∘ ∘ shìr,

帮 我 收拾 房间，好 吗？
bāng ∘ shōushi fángjiān, ∘ ∘?

小明： 哦，……我们 没 空儿，
Ò,… ∘ ∘ ∘ kòngr,

我们 要 去 打 球。
∘ ∘ yào qù dǎ qiú.

妈妈： 打 球？
Dǎ qiú?

现在 天气 太 热 了！
◦ ◦ ◦ qì tài rè ◦!

大雷： 没 关系。我 不 怕 热！
◦ Léi: Méi guānxi. ◦ ◦ pà rè!

Notes:

1. *Dà Léi* – like *Xiǎo Míng, Dà Léi* is also used here as a childhood name.

2. *Wǒmen méi kòngr* – Saying *méi kòngr* (没空儿) is the same as saying *méiyǒu kòngr* (没有空儿) The *yǒu* in *méiyǒu* is often dropped in spoken Chinese. Likewise, *méi guānxi* is the same as *méiyǒu guānxi*.

3. *Wǒmen yào qù dǎ qiú* – *Yào* (要) used before a verb has the meaning of 'to want to (do something)' or 'to intend to'. More examples:

   Wǒ xīngqītiān yào qù Běijīng.
   Wǒ yào kàn diànshì.

   What does the speaker in the above examples want or intend to do?

Find the Chinese →
Nǐ tīngdǒng le ma? →
该你了！**(Gāi nǐ le!)** →

说汉语四 (Shuō Hànyǔ 4)

琳达： 喂？
Líndá: Wèi?

彼得： 琳达，我 是 彼得。
Bǐdé: Líndá, ◦ ◦ ◦ ◦.

你 正在 做 什么？

Find the Chinese

I dislike the heat.
If you're not doing anything …
That doesn't matter.
There's nothing to do!
I don't mind the heat.
We haven't got time.
It's too hot!
It's so boring!

你听懂了吗？

(Nǐ tīngdǒng le ma?)

1. Which is true?
   The woman had intended to
   a) go for a swim
   b) go shopping
   c) play tennis
2. a) It was fine today but it will be rainy tomorrow.
   b) It rained today and it will continue rainy tomorrow.
   c) It was rainy today but it will be fine tomorrow.
3. The weather will
   a) change for the better
   b) be worse
   c) be the same for a few more days

该你了！ (Gāi nǐ le!)

Role play a situation where someone wants you to help do something, e.g.

bāng dìdi zuò zuòyè
bāng tóngxuémen shōushi
jiàoshì

and you make an excuse, e.g.

… méi kòngr … yào qù …

琳达： 我 正在 看 电视 呢。
Líndá: 。 。 。 。 diànshì 。

彼得： 咱们 去 游泳，好 吗？
Bǐdé: Zán 。 qù yóuyǒng, 。 。?

琳达： 游泳？
Líndá: Yóuyǒng?

现在 刮 大 风。
。 。 guā 。 fēng.

彼得： 咳，刮 风 怕 什么？
Bǐdé: Hāi, guā fēng pà 。 。?

琳达： 太 冷 了，我 怕 冷。
Líndá: Tài lěng 。, 。 pà lěng.

Notes:
Wǒ zhèngzài kàn diànshì ne – The *ne* (呢) at the end of this sentence indicates that the action is continuing. Note that it appears together with *zhèngzài* (正在), which also indicates that the action is countinuing, in the sentence. As *ne* and *zhèngzài* have the same function, they can also be used by themselves.

So, to indicate that someone is watching television, you may say any one of the following:

using *zhèngzài*	*Tā* ***zhèngzài*** *kàn diànshì.*
using *ne*	*Tā kàn diànshì* **ne.**
using both	*Tā* ***zhèngzài*** *kàn diànshì* **ne.**

Find the Chinese →

LEARN TO READ page 142

LEARN TO WRITE Lesson Fourteen page 152

Find the Chinese

I'm watching TV.
It's very windy.
I hate the cold.
How about going swimming?
So what if it's windy?

学会认字 (Xuéhuì rèn zì)

4.1

Before reading the text, listen to the recording and answer the questions.

True or false?
1. The woman knows the two men very well.
2. One of the men told her that her watch was slow.
3. One of the men had an inaccurate watch.
4. The woman did not think it was so late.

汉字表 (Hànzì biǎo)

			As in
现	xiàn	*now*	现在
在	zài	*at, in, on*	
点	diǎn	*o'clock*	四点
半	bàn	*half*	六点半
午	wǔ	*noon; midday*	下午
表	biǎo	*wristwatch*	我的表
慢	màn	*slow*	慢了
分	fēn	*minute*	八点十分

Text

W: 请问，现在几点了？

M1: 十二点半。

M2: 不对，你的表慢了，
现在是下午一点十五分了。

W: 一点十五分了！
谢谢你们！

M2: 不谢。

动动脑筋！

(Dòngdong nǎojīn!)

See if you can guess what this word might mean. It is made up of characters you know.

半天

4.2

Before reading the text, listen to the recording and answer the questions.

True or false?
1. The narrator's surname is Fang.
2. He gets up at 6 o'clock and goes to bed at 10 o'clock.
3. He finishes school at around 4 o'clock.

汉字表 (Hànzì biǎo)

			As in
每	měi	*every*	每天
早	zǎo	*early*	早上
起	qǐ	*to rise, get up*	起床
床	chuáng	*bed*	
吃	chī	*to eat*	吃饭
饭	fàn	*meal*	午饭
放	fàng	*to let go, release*	放学
回	huí	*to return*	回家
晚	wǎn	*evening; late*	晚上
做	zuò	*to do, make*	做作业
作	zuò	*to do, act*	作业
业	yè	*(as in zuòyè)*	
睡	shuì	*to sleep*	睡觉
觉	jiào	*sleep*	

动动脑筋！

(Dòngdong nǎojīn!)

See if you can guess what these words might mean. They are made up of characters you know.

小吃
回国
回请
睡午觉
睡大觉

Text

《我的一天》

我叫谢生方。我今年十四岁。我上中学。

我每天早上六点起床，七点上学，中午十二点半吃午饭。

下午四点半我放学回家。
晚上七点做作业，十点睡觉。

4.3

Before reading the text, listen to the recording and answer the questions.

True or false?
1. The boy generally goes home by bike.
2. The boy is walking home because Xiao Ming has his bike.
3. They are both going home by bus.

汉字表 (Hànzì biǎo)

			As in
自	zì	*self*	自行车
行	xíng	*to walk, travel, move*	
车	chē	*vehicle*	
走	zǒu	*to walk*	走路
路	lù	*road, way*	
坐	zuò	*to sit; to travel by ...*	坐车

Text

G: 你的自行车呢？
B: 我借给小明了。
G: 那你今天怎么回家呢？
B: 我今天走路回家，你呢？
G: 我坐车回家。

动动脑筋！
(Dòngdong nǎojīn!)

See if you can guess what these words might mean. They are made up of characters you know.

慢车
快车
小路
问路
同路

4.4

Before reading the text, listen to the recording and answer the questions.

True or false?
1. Xiao Ming was doing his homework at around 10 a.m.
2. Xiao Ming is slightly behind in finishing his homework.
3. He usually gets up at 8:00 every morning.

汉表字 (Hànzì biǎo)

			As in
书	shū	*book*	看书
正	zhèng	*(aspect particle)*	正在
赶	gǎn	*to catch up with; to rush … through*	赶作业
昨	zuó	*yesterday*	昨天

Text

1. 妹妹： 现在十点了，
   你还在看书！
   小明： 我正在赶作业呢！
   妹妹： 什么作业？
   小明： 上个星期的作业。

2. 妈妈： 小明呢？
   妹妹： 他还在睡觉。
   妈妈： 八点了，
   他还在睡觉?!
   妹妹： 他昨天晚上赶作业了。

动动脑筋！

(Dòngdong nǎojīn!)

See if you can guess what this word might mean. It is made up of characters you know.

赶车

Notes:
1. *Tā hái zài kàn shū. Tā hái zài shuìjiào.* – To indicate that something is *still* (还) happening we say *hái zài ...* rather than *hái zhèngzài.*
2. *Shàng gè xīngqī de zuòyè* means 'last week's homework'.
3. *Tā zuótiān wǎnshang gǎn zuòyè le* – *Le* indicates the completion of the action, i.e. that Xiao Ming had started doing his homework and had finished it.

4.5

Before reading the text, listen to the recording and answer the questions.

Dialogue 1:
True or false?
1. There are two teachers surnamed Lin at the school.
2. Both of them teach Chinese language.
3. One of them is in Beijing.
4. Beijing is extremely cold in January.

Dialogue 2:
True or false?
1. It was a hot day.
2. The boys felt that it was too hot to play football.
3. The boy's mother asked them to help her do some work.

汉字表 (Hànzì biǎo)

			As in
冷	lěng	*cold*	很冷
咱	zán	*we (including listener)*	咱们
去	qù	*to go*	去打球
打	dǎ	*to play (ball games)*	打球
球	qiú	*ball*	
气	qì	*air*	天气
热	rè	*hot*	很热
怕	pà	*to fear, dislike*	怕冷
事	shì	*affair, business*	有事儿
儿	er	*(retroflex ending)*	事儿
帮	bāng	*to help*	帮我……

Text

1. B: 你知道吗？
   林老师下星期去北京。
   G: 林老师？哪个林老师？
   B: 我们的汉语老师。
   G: 现在是一月，她现在去北京？
   北京可冷了！
   B: 你怕冷，她可不怕冷！

2. 哥哥： 咱们去打球，好吗？
   弟弟： 今天天气挺热的，
   我不去，我怕热。
   妈妈： 你们没事儿，
   帮我做一点事儿，好吗？
   哥哥： 我们有事儿……
   弟弟： 我们要去打球。
   妈妈： 去打球？
   现在天气很热……
   弟弟： 不热，不热。
   我不怕热！
   哥哥： 我也不怕热！
   弟弟： 走，我们现在去打球。
   哥哥： 走！
   ……
   妈妈： 不怕热？
   你们怕帮妈妈做事儿！

动动脑筋！

(Dòngdong nǎojīn!)

See if you can guess what these words might mean. They are made up of characters you know.

冷气
气球
同事
热狗
怕事儿
国事

Summary

4.1 What's the time?

Now you can:

ask someone the time:
(Láo jià,) xiànzài jǐ diǎn? (劳驾,) 现在几点?

possible replies:
Xiànzài shí diǎn. 现在十点。
Bā diǎn sānshíwǔ fēn. 八点三十五分。
Jiǔ diǎn bàn. 九点半。
Bā diǎn líng wǔ fēn. 八点零五分。
Bā diǎn yí kè. 八点一刻。
Bā diǎn sān kè. 八点三刻。

express a.m. and p.m.:
zǎoshang liù diǎn 早上六点
shàngwǔ jiǔ diǎn 上午九点
xiàwǔ sān diǎn 下午三点
wǎnshang shíyī diǎn 晚上十一点

say your watch is slow:
Wǒ de biǎo màn le. 我的表慢了。

say you are late:
Zánmen wǎn le! 咱们晚了!

urge your companion(s) to hurry:
Zánmen kuài zǒu ba! 咱们快走吧!

Grammar and usage reference
Zǎoshang (早上) and *shàngwǔ* (上午) page 117
Zánmen (咱们) page 119

4.2 Daily routine

Now you can:

describe your daily routine:
Wǒ zǎoshang liù diǎn qǐchuáng. 我早上六点起床。
Wǒ qī diǎn bàn qù shàngxué. 我七点半去上学。
Wǒ sān diǎn wǔshí fēn fàngxué huí jiā. 我三点五十分放学回家。
Wǒ wǎnshang shí diǎn shuìjiào. 我晚上十点睡觉。

describe what you do sometimes:
Wǒ yǒu shíhou kàn shū, yǒu shíhou kàn diànshì.
我有时候看书，有时候看电视。

describe what you do regularly:
Wǒ měi tiān qī diǎn qǐchuáng. 我每天七点起床。

describe the sequence of your actions:
Wǒ liù diǎn chī wǎnfàn, ránhòu zuò zuòyè.
我六点吃晚饭，然后做作业。

4.3 Shall we go by bus?

Now you can:

ask by what means of transport someone goes somewhere:
Tā zěnme huí jiā? 他怎么回家？
Tā zěnme shàngxué? 她怎么上学？

describe how someone goes somewhere:
Lǐ Yún qí chē shàngxué. 李云骑车上学。
Zhāng Jiàn de bàba zuò gōnggòng qìchē shàngbān.
张建的爸爸坐公共汽车上班。
Tā měi tiān zǒu lù huí jiā. 他每天走路回家。

urge someone to hurry:
Kuài yìdiǎnr! 快一点儿！
Kuài, zánmen zǒu ba! 快，咱们走吧！

make a suggestion:
Zánmen zuò gōnggòng qìchē ba!
咱们坐公共汽车吧！

ask about something:
Nǐ de zìxíngchē ne? 你的自行车呢？

Grammar and vocabulary reference
Chē (车) in terms for vehicles page 124
Zuò chē (坐车) and *qí chē* (骑车) page 124
Tài … le (太……了) page 126

4.4 What are they doing?

Now you can:

say what someone is (in the process of) doing:
Liú Xīn zhèngzài tīng yīnyuè. 刘新正在听音乐。
Zhāng Jiàn zhèngzài gǎn zuòyè. 张建正在赶作业。

ask someone who they want:
Nǐ zhǎo shéi? 你找谁?

answer the telephone:
Wèi? 喂?

suggest doing an activity:
Xiàwǔ zánmen qù dǎ qiú, hǎo ma?
下午咱们去打球，好吗?

Useful expressions
Nà hǎo … (那好……) *All right then … (agreeing to someone's suggestion)*
Yíhuìr jiàn! (一会儿见!) *See you soon!*
Nǐ zháo shénme jí? (你着什么急?) *What's the rush/panic?*
Tā lèi le. (她累了。) *She's tired.*
Tā è le. (他饿了。) *He's hungry.*

Grammar and usage reference
Le (了) indicating a change in the situation page 128
Replying to a question which contains *zhèngzài* (正在) page 129
Xiǎo Míng (小明) childhood name page 131
Wèi (喂) used on the telephone page 131

4.5 What's the weather like?

Now you can:

describe the weather:
Jīntiān tiānqì tǐng hǎo de. 今天天气挺好的。
Jīntiān tiānqì hěn lěng. 今天天气很冷。
Xiànzài guā fēng. 现在刮风。
Xiànzài xià yǔ. 现在下雨。

say you dislike or feel the heat or the cold:
Wǒ pà rè. 我怕热。
Wǒ pà lěng. 我怕冷。

suggest doing something:
Zánmen qù dǎ qiú ba! 咱们去打球吧!

ask someone to help you do something:
Bāng wǒ shōushi fángjiān, hǎo ma? 帮我收拾房间，好吗?

say you want (or intend) to do something:
Wǒmen yào qù dǎ qiú. 我们要去打球。

describe what you are in the middle of doing:
Wǒ zhèngzài kàn diànshì ne. 我正在看电视呢。

Useful expressions
Zǒu! (走) *Let's go!*
méi(yǒu) shìr (没(有)事儿) *be free, have nothing on (to do)*
méi(yǒu) kòngr (没(有)空儿) *be occupied, have no time (to do something)*
Zhēn shì wúliáo! (真是无聊!) *It's so boring!*
Méi shìr gàn! (没事儿干!) *Nothing to do!*

Grammar and usage reference
Méi (没) as an abbreviation of *méiyǒu* (没有) page 136
Yào (要) page 136
Zhèngzài ... ne (正在……呢) indicating action is continuing page 137

学会写字 第十一课 (Xuéhuì xiě zì Dì-shíyī kè)

汉字表 (Hànzì biǎo)

现	xiàn *now*	在	zài *at; in*
点	diǎn *o'clock; dot*	午	wǔ *noon, midday*
分	fēn *minute*	半	bàn *half*

Text

a) A: 现在几点？
   B: 现在六点。

b) A: 现在几点？
   B: 现在九点二十五分。

c) A: 现在几点？
   B: 现在上午十点半。

学会写字 第十二课 (Xuéhuì xiě zì Dì-shí'èr kè)

《我的一天》

a)

汉字表 (Hànzì biǎo)

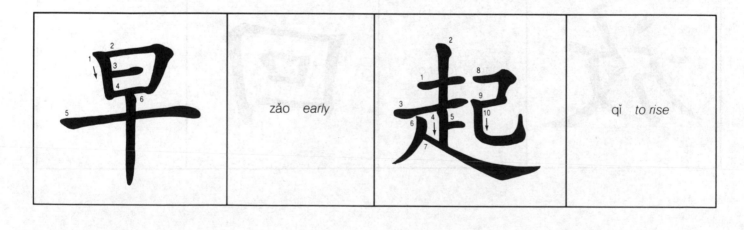

早	zǎo *early*	起	qǐ *to rise*

床	chuáng *bed*

Text

我叫…… .
我今年十四岁。我上中学。
我早上六点起床，
七点上学。

学会写字 第十三课 (Xuéhuì xiě zì Dì-shísān kè)

汉字表 (Hànzì biǎo)

放	fàng *to let go*	回	huí *to return*

晚	wǎn *evening*	睡	*shuì* *to sleep*
觉	jiào *sleep*		

Text

下午四点半我放学回家。
我晚上九点睡觉。

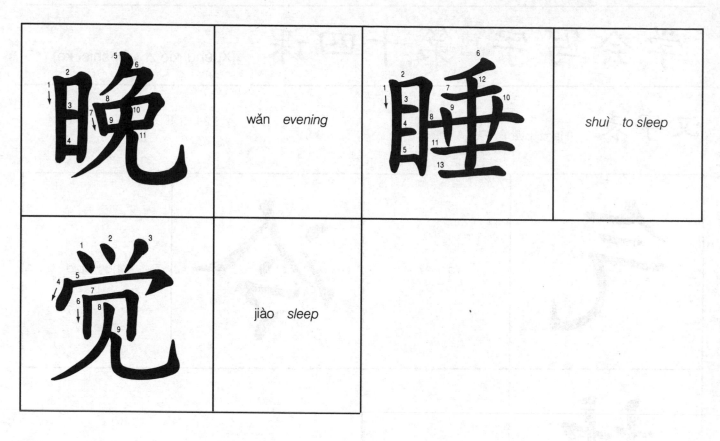

学会写字 第十四课 (Xuéhuì xiě zì Dì-shísì kè)

汉字表 (Hànzì biǎo)

气	qì *air*	冷	lěng *cold*
热	rè *hot*		

Text

今天是九月二十八号星期天。
天气很好，不冷也不热。

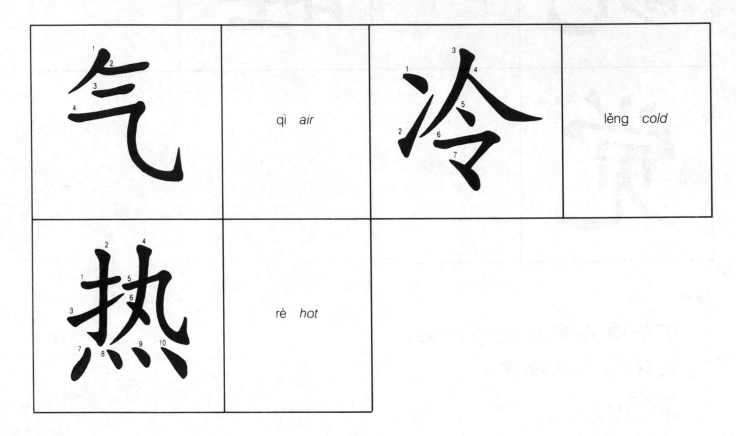

Unit vocabulary

Unit 1 你好！ (Hello!)

dānyuán 单元 *unit*
dì-yī 第一 *first*

1.1 中国－汉语 Zhōngguó – Hànyǔ

Hànyǔ 汉语 *Chinese language*
Zhōngguó 中国 *China*

1.2 Hello!

bàba 爸爸 *father*
Bǐdé 彼得 *Peter*
hǎo 好 *good;well*
lǎoshī 老师 *teacher*
māma 妈妈 *mother*
nǐ 你 *you (singular)*
  nǐmen 你们 *you (plural)*
  Nǐ tīngdǒng le ma? 你听懂了吗? *(listening) Did you understand?*
nín 您 *you (polite)*
tóngxué 同学 *fellow student*
  tóngxuémen 同学们 *fellow students*
zàijiàn 再见 *goodbye*

Learn to read

biǎo 表 *table; list*
dòng 动 *move*
Hànzì 汉字 *Chinese character*
nǎojīn 脑筋 *brains; mind*
rèn 认 *recognise; identify*
xuéhuì 学会 *learn; master*
zì 字 *character; word*

Learn to write

kè 课 *lesson*
xiě 写 *write*

1.3 How are you?

ba 吧 *(modal particle)*
Gāi nǐ le. 该你了。 *It's your turn.*
hái kěyǐ 还可以 *all right; so so*
Jiànhuá 建华 *(given name)*
jìn 进 *to enter*
Lín Fāng 林方 *(name)*
ma 吗 *(question particle)*
Mǎlì 玛丽 *Mary*
ne 呢 *(modal particle)*
Nǐ hǎo ma? 你好吗? *How are you?*
Nǐ zěnmeyàng 你怎么样 *How are things with you?*
qǐng 请 *Please*
shuō 说 *to say; to speak*
tǐng hǎo de 挺好的 *quite good*
wèi 喂 *hello; hey*
xiè 谢 *to thank*
  xièxie 谢谢 *thank you*
yě 也 *also*
yī 一 *one*
Zhāng Jiànhuá 张建华 *(name)*
zuò 坐 *to sit*

1.4 What is your name?

Ānnà 安娜 *Anna*
  Ānnà dè 安娜的 *Anna's*
bù 不 *not*
de 的 *(particle indicating the possessive)*
Hànyǔ lǎoshī 汉语老师 *Chinese language teacher*
jiào 叫 *to be called*
Lǐ Guóhuá 李国华 *(name)*
Lín 林 *(family name)*
Líndá 琳达 *Linda*
míngzi 名字 *name*
nǐ de 你的 *your, yours*
  nǐmen de 你们的 *your, yours (plural)*
Nín guì xìng? 您贵姓? *(polite way of asking someone's family name)*
péngyou 朋友 *friend*
Qǐngwèn … 请问…… *Please may I ask …*
shéi 谁 *who*
shénme 什么 *what*
shì 是 *am, are, is*
Shǐmìsī 史密斯 *Smith*
tā 他 *he; him*
  tā de 他的 *his*
  tāmen 他们 *they; them*
  tāmen de 他们的 *their, theirs*
tā 她 *she; her*
  tā 她的 *her, hers*
wèn 问 *to ask*
wǒ 我 *I; me*
  wǒ de 我的 *my, mine*
  wǒmen de 我们的 *our, ours*
xìng 姓 *surname; to be surnamed*
xuésheng 学生 *student*
Zhāng 张 *(family name)*

Learn to write

dì-èr 第二 *second*

1.5 What country are you from?

Àodàlìyàrén 澳大利亚人 *Australian (person)*
duìbuqǐ 对不起 *sorry (apology)*
èr 二 *two*
guó 国 *country, nation*
méi guānxi 没关系 *never mind*
něi 哪 *which*
Ò 哦 *(exclamation expressing understanding or realisation)*
rén 人 *person; people*
Rìběnrén 日本人 *Japanese (person)*
wǒmen 我们 *we; us*
xué 学 *to study*
Zhōngguórén 中国人 *Chinese (person)*

Learn to read

dòng 动 *move*
nǎojīn 脑筋 *brains; mind*

Learn to write

dì-sān 第三 *third*

Unit 2 我的一家 (Meet my family)

yì jiā 一家 *(whole) family*

2.1 Meet my family

Běijīng 北京 *Beijing (Peking)*
Dàwèi 大卫 *David*
dà 大 *big*
  dàxué 大学 *university*
  dàxuéshēng 大学生 *university student*
dìdi 弟弟 *younger brother*
gēge 哥哥 *elder brother*
Guǎngzhōu 广州 *Guangzhou (Canton)*
Huāzǐ 花子 *Hanako*
jiějie 姐姐 *elder sister*
jièshào 介绍 *to introduce*
lái 来 *(as in lái jièshào; indicating intention to do something)*
Mǎdīng 马丁 *Martin*
mèimei 妹妹 *younger sister*
Mò'ěrběn 墨尔本 *Melbourne*
nà 那 *that*
nǎr 哪儿 *where*
shàng 上 *to attend (school)*
Xīní 悉尼 *Sydney*
xiǎo 小 *small*
  xiǎoxué 小学 *primary school*
yíxià 一下 *(adds informality to tone)*
Zhào Qīng 赵青 *(name)*
Zhào Wén 赵文 *(name)*
Zhào Yuǎn 赵远 *(name)*
Zhào Yún 赵云 *(name)*
Zhāng Jiànqiū 张建秋 *(name)*
Zhēnní 珍妮 *Jenny*
zhè 这 *this*
zhōngxué 中学 *high school*
zhù 住 *to live*

Learn to write

dì-sì 第四 *fourth*

2.2 My family

Ālún 阿伦 *Alan*
bā 八 *eight*
gè 个 *(general measure word)*
hái 还 *still, even; also, too, in addition, as well*
  hái yǒu 还有 *also; furthermore*
hé 和 *and; with*
jǐ 几 *how many*
jiā 家 *family*
jiǔ 九 *nine*
Lǐ 李 *(family name)*
liǎng 两 *two (of something)*
liù 六 *six*
méi(yǒu) 没（有） *do not have; there is not; not*
nǎinai 奶奶 *(paternal) grandmother*
qī 七 *seven*
sān 三 *three*
shí 十 *ten*
sì 四 *four*
wǔ 五 *five*
xiōngdì jiěmèi 兄弟姐妹 *brothers and sisters*
yǒu 有 *to have; there is, there are*
Zhāng Léi 张雷 *(name)*
Zhào Míng 赵明 *(name)*
zhǐ 只 *only; merely*
  zhǐ yǒu 只有 *only have …*

Learn to write

dì-wǔ 第五 *fifth*

2.3 I have a pet!

dòngwù 动物 *animal*
Fēifei 非非 *(name)*
gǒu 狗 *dog*
jīnyú 金鱼 *(gold)fish*
le 了 *(particle indicating that the action has happened)*
mǎ 马 *horse*
māo 猫 *cat*
Mīmi 咪咪 *(name)*
niǎo 鸟 *bird*
pǐ 匹 *(MW for horse)*
tā 它 *it*
tiáo 条 *(MW for fish)*
yǎng 养 *to keep, raise*
xiǎo māo 小猫 *kitten*
zhī 只 *(MW for dog, cat etc)*

Learn to read

Lìlì 利利 *(name)*

Learn to write

dì-liù 第六 *sixth*

2.4 Describing your pet

a 啊 *(particle indicating an exclamation)*
ǎi 矮 *(of height) short*
Āiyō 哎哟 *(exclamation expressing surprise, pain) Oh*
dǎjià 打架 *to fight*
duì 对 *correct; right*
féi 肥 *(of animals) fat*
gāo 高 *high; tall*
hǎokàn 好看 *good looking, attractive*
hǎowánr 好玩儿 *fun; amusing*
hěn 很 *very*
kě ... le 可......了 *extremely; very*
Mǎkè 马克 *Mark*
nèi 那 *that*
pàng 胖 *(of people) fat*
piàoliang 漂亮 *attractive; beautiful*
shòu 瘦 *thin*
táoqì 淘气 *naughty; mischievous*
tǐng ... de 挺......的 *quite ...; very ...; rather ...*
xiǎo gǒu 小狗 *puppy*
yáng 羊 *sheep; goat*
yǐwéi 以为 *to think (mistakenly)*
yǒu yìsi 有意思 *interesting*
yú 鱼 *fish*
zhèi 这 *this*
zhēn 真 *really; true*

Learn to read

Dàtóng 大同 *(name)*

2.5 More counting: 11 to 99

duōshao 多少 *how many*
háishi 还是 *or*
jiā 加 *to add*
liàn 练 *to practise*
  liàn yí liàn 练一练 *(a more casual way of saying 'liàn')*
nán 难 *difficult*
jiǎn 减 *to subtract*
róngyì 容易 *easy*

2.6 How old are you?

duō dà? 多大？ *how old?*
kuài ... le 快...... *soon ...; nearly ...*
le 了 *(particle indicating that a change has taken place)*
suì 岁 *years of age*
Wáng 王 *(surname)*
xiānsheng 先生 *Mr; gentleman*
tàitai 太太 *Mrs; wife*
xiǎojie 小姐 *Miss; young lady*
zhīdao 知道 *to know*

Learn to read

Duì le, ... 对了，...... *That's right, ...*
Wáng Hànshēng 王汉生 *(name)*

Learn to write

dì-qī 第七 *seventh*

Unit 3 上课了！ (Our classroom)

shàngkè 上课 *attend class*
  Shàngkè le! 上课了！ *(said by teacher when class begins) Let's begin!*

3.1 Our classroom

fángjiān 房间 *room*
Huáng 黄 *(surname)*
jiā 家 *home*
jiàoshì 教室 *classroom*
Lín Lánlán 林兰兰 *(name)*
shūbāo 书包 *schoolbag*
Wáng Huá 王华 *(name)*
xuéxiào 学校 *school*
Yīngyǔ 英语 *English language*
  Yīngyǔ lǎoshī 英语老师 *English language teacher*
zhuōzi 桌子 *table*

Learn to write

dì-bā 第八 *eighth*

3.2 Whose is it?

bǐ 笔 *writing instrument*
Bú xiè. 不谢。*(polite response) Don't mention it.*
búyòng 不用 *need not*
  Búyòng kèqi. 不用客气。*(polite response) Not at all. Don't mention it.*
diū 丢 *to lose*
  diū le 丢了 *be lost*
gěi 给 *to give*
huà(r) 画（儿） *picture*
jiǎn 捡 *to pick up*
  jiǎndào 捡到 *picked up*
kàn 看 *to see; look*
  kànkan 看看 *have a look*
kèqi 客气 *courtesy; politeness*
Láolā 劳拉 *Laura*
qiú 球 *ball*
shéi de 谁的 *whose*
shū 书 *book*
zhī 支 *(MW for pencil, pen etc)*
zìxíngchē 自行车 *bicycle*

Learn to read

Wáng Lì 王利 *(name)*

Learn to write

dì-jiǔ 第九 *ninth*

3.3 How do you say it?

dàjiā 大家 *everyone*
chǐzi 尺子 *ruler*
dìtú 地图 *map*
dǒng 懂 *to understand*
hēibǎn 黑板 *blackboard*
kèběn 课本 *text book*
Lǐ Míng 李明 *(name)*
liànxíběn 练习本 *exercise book*
Ó 哦 *(exclamation expressing doubt)*
xiàkè 下课 *to finish class*
xiàngpí 橡皮 *eraser; rubber*
Yīngwén 英文 *English language*
yǐzi 椅子 *chair*
Zài shuō yí biàn. 再说一遍。*Please say it once more.*
zěnme 怎么 *how*
Zhōngwén 中文 *Chinese language*

Learn to read

Duì le! 对了！ *That's right!*

3.4 Which one is it?

bǎ 把 *(MW for chair, ruler)*
běn 本 *(MW for book, novel)*
dōngxi 东西 *thing*
Hǎo. 好。*All right. (agreeing to something)*
  …, hǎo ma? …, 好吗？ *Is it all right if I …? (making a request)*
  hǎokàn 好看 *good to read*
jiè 借 *to borrow; to lend*
  jiè(gěi) 借（给） *lend to (someone)*
kuài 块 *(MW for blackboard, rubber)*
liàng 辆 *(MW for bicycle, vehicles)*
nèige 那个 *that (one)*
  nèixiē 那些 *those (ones)*
xiǎoshuō 小说 *novel*
xiē 些 *several*
yào 要 *to want*
Zhāng Yún 张云 *(name)*
zhāng 张 *(MW for table)*
zhèige 这个 *this (one)*
  zhèixiē 这些 *these (ones)*

3.5 What day is today?

hào 号 *date; number*
hòutiān 后天 *day after tomorrow*
jīnnián 今年 *this year*
…jiàn! ……见！ *See you …!*

jīntiān 今天 *today*
liùyuè 六月 *June*
míngnián 明年 *next year*
míngtiān 明天 *tomorrow*
nián 年 *year*
qùnián 去年 *last year*
shàng gè xīngqī 上个星期 *last week*
  shàng gè yuè 上个月 *last month*
sìyuè 四月 *April*
tiān 天 *day; sky; heaven*
xīngqī 星期 *week*
xīngqī'èr 星期二 *Tuesday*
  xīngqīliù 星期六 *Saturday*
  xīngqīsān 星期三 *Wednesday*
  xīngqīsì 星期四 *Thursday*
  xīngqītiān 星期天 *Sunday*
  xīngqīwǔ 星期五 *Friday*
  xīngqīyī 星期一 *Monday*
xià gè xīngqī 下个星期 *next week*
xià gè yuè 下个月 *next month*
yīyuè 一月 *January*
yuè 月 *month*
zhèige xīngqī 这个星期 *this week*
  zhèige yuè 这个月 *this month*
zuótiān 昨天 *yesterday*

3.6 Today is my birthday

… ba? ……吧? *(asking for confirmation)*
chàng 唱 *to sing*
  chàng yí chàng 唱一唱 *(a more casual way of saying 'chàng')*
hēibǎn shàng 黑板上 *on the blackboard*
kuàilè 快乐 *happy*
nà 那 *then; in that case*
shēngrì 生日 *birthday*
Shì ma? 是吗? *Is that so? Is it?*
xiězài … shàng 写在……上 *to write on … (something)*
zhù 祝…… *to wish (someone) …*

Learn to write

dì-shí 第十 *tenth*

Unit 4 我的一天 (Daily routine)

4.1 What is the time?

bàn 半 *half*
biǎo 表 *watch*
diǎn 点 *o'clock*
fēn 分 *minute*
kè 刻 *quarter (of an hour)*
kuài 快 *quick*
Láo jià, … 劳驾,…… *Excuse me, …; Would you mind ….*
líng 零 *nought*
màn 慢 *slow*
  màn le 慢了 *to be slow*
shàngwǔ 上午 *morning*
xiàwǔ 下午 *afternoon*
wǎn 晚 *late*
  wǎn le 晚了 *to be late*
  wǎnshang 晚上 *evening*
xiànzài 现在 *now*
zánmen 咱们 *we; us (includes listener)*
zǎoshang 早上 *morning*
zhōngwǔ 中午 *noon, midday*
zǒu 走 *to walk; to leave*

Learn to write

dì-shíyī 第十一 *eleventh*

4.2 Daily routine

cāo 操 *drill; set physical exercise*
chī 吃 *to eat*
chuáng 床 *bed*
dǎ 打 *to play (sport)*
  dǎ qiú 打球 *to play ball games (except football)*
diànshì 电视 *television*
fàn 饭 *food; cooked rice*
fàngxué 放学 *to finish school for the day*
huí 回 *to return*
  huí jiā 回家 *to return home*
kàn 看 *to read; to watch*
  kàn shū 看书 *to read (a book)*
  kàn diànshì 看电视 *to watch television*
kèjiān 课间 *break between classes at school*
  kèjiāncāo 课间操 *set physical exercises during break*
Línglíng 玲玲 *(name)*
měi 每 *every*
  měi tiān 每天 *every day*
qǐ 起 *to rise*
  qǐchuáng 起床 *to get out of bed*
qù 去 *to go*
ránhòu 然后 *then; after that*
shàngxué 上学 *to go to school*
shíhou 时候 *time*
shuìjiào 睡觉 *to sleep*

wǎnfàn 晚饭 *evening meal*
wǔfàn 午饭 *lunch*
yǒu shíhou 有时候 *sometimes*
zǎofàn 早饭 *breakfast*
zuò 做 *to do*
  zuò kèjiāncāo 做课间操 *to do set physical exercises*
  zuò zuòyè 做作业 *to do homework*
zuòyè 作业 *homework*

Learn to read

Xiè Shēngfāng 谢生方 *(name)*

Learn to write

dì-shí'èr 第十二 *twelfth*

4.3 Shall we go by bus?

chē 车 *vehicle*
diànchē 电车 *tram*
gōnggòng qìchē 公共汽车 *bus*
huǒchē 火车 *train*
Lǐ Yún 李云 *(name)*
lù 路 *road*
mótuōchē 摩托车 *motorbike*
Nǐ zháo shénme jí? 你着什么急? *What are you worried/ anxious about?*
qí 骑 *to ride (astride)*
  qí zìxíngchē 骑自行车 *to ride a bicycle*
  qí chē 骑车 *to ride a bicycle*
  qí mǎ 骑马 *to ride a horse*
qìchē 汽车 *car; bus; truck etc.*
shàngbān 上班 *to go to work; to be at work*
tài … le 太……了 *extremely …; too …*
yìdiǎnr 一点儿 *a little*
Zhāng Jiàn 张建 *(name)*
zǒu lù 走路 *to walk*
zuò 坐 *to travel by*
  zuò chē 坐车 *to travel by bus, car, train*

Learn to write

dì -shísān 第十三 *thirteenth*

4.4 What are they doing?

Bǎoluó 保罗 *Paul*
Bái Yún 白云 *(name)*
děng 等 *to wait*
duō 多 *many*
è 饿 *hungry; to be hungry*
gǎn 赶 *to catch up with; to rush … through*
  gǎn zuòyè 赶作业 *to catch up with homework*
…, hǎo ma? ……,好吗? *Shall we …? How about …?*
huà 画 *to draw; to paint*
lèi 累 *tired; to be tired*
Liú Fāng 刘方 *(name)*
Liú Xīn 刘新 *(name)*
Nà hǎo,… 那好,…… *All right then, … (agreeing to a suggestion)*
qiúmí 球迷 *someone who loves to play or watch ball games*
tīng 听 *to listen*
Wáng Shū 王书 *(name)*
Wáng Yún 王云 *(name)*
Xiǎo Míng 小明 *(name)*
xìn 信 *letter*
yáogǔnyuè 摇滚乐 *rock music*
yíhuìr 一会儿 *a short while*
yīnyuè 音乐 *music*
zhǎo 找 *to look for*
  zhǎo péngyou 找朋友 *to go to see friends*
zháojí 着急 *to worry, feel anxious*
zhèng(zài) 正(在) *(aspect particle); in the process of*

4.5 What's the weather like?

bāng 帮 *to help*
Dà Léi 大雷 *(name)*
fēng 风 *wind*
Hāi 咳 *(exclamation indicating surprise, disdain, regret)*
gàn 干 *to do*
guā 刮 *to blow (of wind)*
  guā fēng 刮风 *to be windy*
kòngr 空儿 *free time*
lěng 冷 *cold*
méi kòngr 没空儿 *not free; have no time*
pà 怕 *to fear*
  pà lěng 怕冷 *to dislike or feel the cold*
  pà rè 怕热 *to dislike or feel the heat*
rè 热 *hot*
shì(r) 事(儿) *affair; matter*
shōushi 收拾 *to tidy up*
tiānqì 天气 *weather*
wúliáo 无聊 *bored*
xià 下 *to fall (of rain, snow, hail)*
  xià yǔ 下雨 *to rain*
yào 要 *to want; to intend*
yǒu shìr 有事儿 *to be busy; to have something on*
yǒu kòngr 有空儿 *to be free; to have spare time*
yóuyǒng 游泳 *to swim*
yǔ 雨 *rain*
zěnmeyàng 怎么样 *how*

Learn to write

dì-shísì 第十四 *fourteenth*

Vocabulary

1. Single character entries are listed in alphabetical order. Characters with the same *pinyin* spelling but different tone are arranged according to tone. Characters with both the same spelling and same tone are arranged according to the number of strokes.
   Compounds listed under their respective single-character entries are arranged alphabetically according to the second character of the compound.
2. Compounds not listed under single-character entries are arranged in alphabetical order.
3. LTR = Learn to Read; LTW = Learn to Write.

A

- a 啊 *(particle indicating an exclamation)* 2.4
- ǎi 矮 *(of height) short* 2.4
- Āiyō 哎哟 *(exclamation expressing surprise, pain) Oh* 2.4
- Ālún 阿伦 *Alan* 2.2
- Ānnà 安娜 *Anna* 1.4
  - Ānna dè 安娜的 *Anna's* 1.4
- Àodàlìyàrén 澳大利亚人 *Australian (person)* 1.5

B

- bā 八 *eight* 2.2
- bǎ 把 *(MW for chair, ruler)* 3.4
- bàba 爸爸 *father* 1.2
- ba 吧 *(modal particle)* 1.3
- ... ba? ……吧? *(asking for confirmation)* 3.6
- Bái Yún 白云 *(name)* 4.4
- bàn 半 *half* 4.1
- bāng 帮 *to help* 4.5
- Bǎoluó 保罗 *Paul* 4.4
- Běijīng 北京 *Beijing (Peking)* 2.1
- běn 本 *(MW for book, novel)* 3.4
- bǐ 笔 *writing instrument* 3.2
- Bǐdé 彼得 *Peter* 1.2
- biǎo 表 *table; list* LTR 1.1
- biǎo 表 *watch* 4.1
- bù 不 *not* 1.4
  - Bú xiè. 不谢。*(polite response) Don't mention it.* 3.2
  - Búyòng 不用 *need not* 3.2
    - Búyòng kèqi. 不用客气。*(polite response) Not at all. Don't mention it.* 3.2

C

- cāi 猜 *guess* LTR 2.3
- cāo 操 *drill; set physical exercise* 4.2
- chàng 唱 *to sing*
  - chàng yí chàng 唱一唱 *(a more casual way of saying 'chàng')* 4.2
- chē 车 *vehicle* 4.3
- chī 吃 *to eat* 4.2
- chǐzi 尺子 *ruler* 3.3
- chuáng 床 *bed* 4.2

D

- dǎ 打 *to play (sport); to strike* 4.2
  - dǎjià 打架 *to fight* 2.4
  - dǎ qiú 打球 *to play ball games (except football)* 4.2
- dà 大 *big* 2.1
  - dàjiā 大家 *everyone* 3.3
  - Dà Léi 大雷 *(name)* 4.5
  - Dàtóng 大同 *(name)* LTR 2.4
  - Dàwèi 大卫 *David* 2.1
  - dàxué 大学 *university* 2.1
    - dàxuéshēng 大学生 *university student* 2.1
- dānyuán 单元 *unit* 1
- de 的 *(particle indicating the possessive)* 1.4
- děng 等 *to wait* 4.4
- dì-bā 第八 *eighth* LTW 8
- dì-èr 第二 *second* LTW 2
- dì-jiǔ 第九 *ninth* LTW 9
- dì-liù 第六 *sixth* LTW 6
- dì-qī 第七 *seventh* LTW 7
- dì-sān 第三 *third* LTW 3
- dì-shí 第十 *tenth* LTW 10
- dì-shí'èr 第十二 *twelfth* LTW 12
- dì-shísān 第十三 *thirteenth* LTW 13
- dì-shísì 第十四 *fourteenth* LTW 14
- dì-shíyī 第十一 *eleventh* LTW 11
- dì-sì 第四 *fourth* LTW 4
- dì-wǔ 第五 *fifth* LTW 5
- dì-yī 第一 *first* 1
- dìdi 弟弟 *younger brother* 2.1
- dìtú 地图 *map* 3.3
- diǎn 点 *o'clock* 4.1
- diànchē 电车 *tram; trolley bus* 4.3
- diànshì 电视 *television* 4.2
- diū 丢 *to lose* 3.2
  - diū le 丢了 *be lost* 3.2
- dōngxi 东西 *thing* 3.4
- dǒng 懂 *to understand* 3.3
- dòng 动 *move* LTR 1.1
  - dòngwù 动物 *animal* 2.3
- duì 对 *correct; right; towards* 2.4
  - Duì le, ... 对了,…… *That's right, ...* LTR 2.6
  - Duì le! 对了! *That's right!* LTR 3.3
  - duìbuqǐ 对不起 *sorry (apology)* 1.5
- duō 多 *many* 4.4
  - duō dà? 多大? *how old?* 2.6
  - duōshao? 多少? *how many* 2.5

E

è 饿 *hungry; to be hungry* 4.4
èr 二 *two* 1.5

F

fàn 饭 *food; cooked rice* 4.2
fángjiān 房间 *room* 3.1
fàngxué 放学 *to finish school for the day* 4.2
féi 肥 *(of animals) fat* 2.4
Fēifei 非非 *(name)* 2.3
fēn 分 *minute* 4.1
fēng 风 *wind* 4.5

G

Gāi nǐ le. 该你了。*It's your turn.* 1.4
gǎn 赶 *to catch up with; to rush … through* 4.4
  gǎn zuòyè 赶作业 *to catch up with homework* 4.4
gàn 干 *to do* 4.5
gāo 高 *high; tall* 2.4
gēge 哥哥 *elder brother* 2.1
gè 个 *(general measure word)* 2.2
gěi 给 *to give* 3.2
gōnggòng qìchē 公共汽车 *bus* 4.3
gǒu 狗 *dog* 2.3
guā 刮 *(of wind) to blow* 4.5
  guā fēng 刮风 *to be windy* 4.5
Guǎngzhōu 广州 *Guangzhou (Canton)* 2.1
guó 国 *country, nation* 1.5

H

Hāi 咳 *(exclamation indicating surprise, disdain, regret)* 4.5
hái 还 *still, even; also, too, in addition, as well* 2.2
  hái kěyǐ 还可以 *all right; so so* 1.3
  hái yǒu 还有 *also; furthermore* 2.2
  háishi 还是 *or* 2.5
hǎo 好 *good; well* 1.2
  Hǎo. 好。*All right. (agreeing to something)* 3.4
  …, hǎo ma? ……，好吗？*Shall we …? How about …?* 4.4
  hǎokàn 好看 *good looking, attractive* 2.4
  hǎokàn 好看 *good to read* 3.4
  hǎowánr 好玩儿 *fun; amusing* 2.4
hào 号 *date; number* 3.5
Hànyǔ 汉语 *Chinese language* 1.1
  Hànyǔ lǎoshī 汉语老师 *Chinese language teacher* 1.4
  Hànzì 汉字 *Chinese character* LTR 1.1
hé 和 *and; with* 2.2
hēibǎn 黑板 *blackboard* 3.3
  hēibǎn shàng 黑板上 *on the blackboard* 3.6
hěn 很 *very* 2.4
hòutiān 后天 *day after tomorrow* 3.5
huà 画 *to draw; to paint* 4.4
  huà(r) 画（儿）*picture* 3.2
Huāzǐ 花子 *Hanako* 2.1
Huáng 黄 *(surname)* 3.1
huí 回 *to return* 4.2
  huí jiā 回家 *to return home* 4.2
huǒchē 火车 *train* 4.3

J

jǐ 几 *how many* 2.2
jiā 加 *to add* 2.5
jiā 家 *family* 2.2
jiā 家 *home* 3.1
jìn 进 *to enter* 1.3
jīnnián 今年 *this year* 3.5
jīntiān 今天 *today* 3.5
jīnyú 金鱼 *(gold)fish* 2.3
jiǎn 捡 *to pick up* 3.2
  jiǎndào 捡到 *picked up* 3.2
jiǎn 减 *to subtract* 2.5
… jiàn! ……见！*See you …!* 3.5
Jiànhuá 建华 *(name)* 1.3
jiào 叫 *to be called* 1.4
jiàoshì 教室 *classroom* 3.1
jiè 借 *to borrow; to lend* 3.4
  jiè(gěi) 借（给）*lend to (someone)* 3.4
jiějie 姐姐 *elder sister* 2.1
jièshào 介绍 *to introduce* 2.1
jiǔ 九 *nine* 2.2

K

kàn 看 *to see; to look; to read; to watch* 3.2
  kàn diànshì 看电视 *to watch television* 4.2
  kàn shū 看书 *to read (a book)* 4.2
  kànkan 看看 *have a look* 3.2
kě … le 可……了 *extremely; very* 2.4
kè 刻 *quarter (of an hour)* 4.1
kè 课 *lesson* LTW 1
  kèběn 课本 *text book* 3.3
  kèjiān 课间 *(break between classes at school)* 4.2
    kèjiāncāo 课间操 *set physical exercises during break* 4.2
kèqi 客气 *courtesy; politeness* 3.2
kòngr 空儿 *free time* 4.5
kuài 块 *(MW for blackboard, rubber)* 3.4
kuài 快 *quick* 4.1
  kuài … le 快……了 *soon …; nearly …* 2.6
  kuàilè 快乐 *happy* 3.6

L

lái 来 *(as in* lái jièshào*; indicating intention to do something)* 2.1
Láo jià, 劳驾，…… *Excuse me, …; Would you mind …?* 4.1
Láolā 劳拉 *Laura* 3.2
lǎoshī 老师 *teacher* 1.2
le 了 *(particle indicating that the action has happened)* 2.3
le 了 *(particle indicating that a change has taken place)* 2.6
lèi 累 *tired; to be tired* 4.4
lěng 冷 *cold* 4.5

Língling 玲玲 *(name)* 4.2
Lǐ 李 *(family name)* 2.2
  Lǐ Guóhuá 李国华 *(name)* 1.4
  Lǐ Míng 李明 *(name)* 3.3
  Lǐ Yún 李云 *(name)* 4.3
Lìlì 利利 *(name)* LTR 2.3
liàn 练 *to practise* 2.5
  liàn yí liàn 练一练 *(a more casual way of saying 'liàn')* 2.5
  liànxíběn 练习本 *exercise book* 3.3
liǎng 两 *two (of something)* 2.2
liàng 辆 *(MW for bicycle, vehicles)* 3.4
Lín 林 *(family name)* 1.4
  Lín Fāng 林方 *(name)* 1.3
  Lín Lánlán 林兰兰 *(name)* 3.1
Líndá 琳达 *Linda* 1.4
líng 零 *nought* 4.1
Liú Fāng 刘方 *(name)* 4.4
Liú Xīn 刘新 *(name)* 4.4
liù 六 *six* 2.2
  liùyuè 六月 *June* 3.5
lù 路 *road* 4.3

M

ma 吗 *(question particle)* 1.3
māma 妈妈 *mother* 1.2
mǎ 马 *horse* 2.3
Mǎdīng 马丁 *Martin* 2.1
Mǎkè 马克 *Mark* 2.4
Mǎlì 玛丽 *Mary* 1.3
màn 慢 *slow* 4.1
  màn le 慢了 *to be slow* 4.1
māo 猫 *cat* 2.3
méi(yǒu) 没（有）*do not have; there is not; not* 2.2
  méi guānxi 没关系 *never mind* 1.5
  méi kòngr 没空儿 *not free; have no time* 4.5
měi 每 *every* 4.2
  měi tiān 每天 *every day* 4.2
mèimei 妹妹 *younger sister* 2.1
Mīmi 咪咪 *(name)* 2.3
míngnián 明年 *next year* 3.5
míngtiān 明天 *tomorrow* 3.5
míngzi 名字 *name* 1.4
Mò'ěrběn 墨尔本 *Melbourne* 2.1
mótuōchē 摩托车 *motorbike* 4.3

N

nà 那 *that* 2.1
nà 那 *then; in that case* 3.6
  Nà hǎo, ... 那好,...... *All right then, ... (agreeing to a suggestion)* 4.4
nǎinai 奶奶 *(paternal) grandmother* 2.2
nán 难 *difficult* 2.5
nǎojīn 脑筋 *brains; mind* LTR 1.1
nǎr 哪儿 *where* 2.1
ne 呢 *(modal particle)* 1.3
něi 哪 *which* 1.5
nèi 那 *that* 2.4
  nèige 那个 *that (one)* 3.4
  nèixiē 那些 *those (ones)* 3.4
nǐ 你 *you (singular)* 1.2
  nǐ de 你的 *your, yours* 1.4
  Nǐ hǎo ma? 你好吗? *How are you?* 1.3
  Nǐ tīngdǒng le ma? 你听懂了吗? *(listening) Did you understand?* 1.2
  Nǐ zěnmeyàng? 你怎么样? *How are things with you?* 1.3
  Nǐ zháo shénme jí? 你着什么急? *What are you worried/anxious about?* 4.3
  nǐmen 你们 *you (plural)* 1.2
  nǐmen de 你们的 *your, yours (plural)* 1.4
nín 您 *you (polite)* 1.2
  Nín guì xìng? 您贵姓 *(polite way of asking someone's family name)* 1.4
nián 年 *year* 3.5
niǎo 鸟 *bird* 2.3

O

Ó 哦 *(exclamation expressing doubt)* 3.3
Ò 哦 *(exclamation expressing understanding or realisation)* 1.5

P

pà 怕 *to fear* 4.5
  pà lěng 怕冷 *to dislike or feel the cold* 4.5
  pà rè 怕热 *to dislike or feel the heat* 4.5
pàng 胖 *(of people)* fat 2.4
péngyou 朋友 *friend* 1.4
pǐ 匹 *(MW for horse)* 2.3
piàoliang 漂亮 *attractive; beautiful* 2.4

Q

qī 七 *seven* 2.2
qí 骑 *to ride (astride)* 4.3
  qí chē 骑车 *to ride a bicycle* 4.3
  qí mǎ 骑马 *to ride a horse* 4.3
  qí zìxíngchē 骑自行车 *to ride a bicycle* 4.3
qǐ 起 *to rise* 4.2
  qǐchuáng 起床 *to get out of bed* 4.2
qìchē 汽车 *car; bus; truck etc.* 4.3
qǐng 请 *please* 1.3
  Qǐngwèn, ... 请问,...... *Please may I ask ...* 1.4
qiú 球 *ball* 3.2
  qiúmí 球迷 *someone who loves to play or watch ball games* 4.4
qù 去 *to go* 4.2
  qùnián 去年 *last year* 3.5

R

ránhòu 然后 *then; after that* 4.2
rè 热 *hot* 4.5
rén 人 *person; people* 1.5
rèn 认 *recognise; identify* LTR 1.1
Rìběnrén 日本人 *Japanese (person)* 1.5
róngyì 容易 *easy* 2.5

S

sān 三 *three* 2.2
sì 四 *four* 2.2
  sìyuè 四月 *April* 3.5
shàng 上 *to attend (school); preceding; on, above* 2.1
  shàng gè xīngqī 上个星期 *last week* 3.5
  shàng gè yuè 上个月 *last month* 3.5
  shàngbān 上班 *to go to work; to be at work* 4.3
  shàngkè 上课 *attend class* 3
    Shàngkè le! 上课了！ *(said by teacher when class begins) Let's begin!* 3
  shàngwǔ 上午 *morning* 4.1
  shàngxué 上学 *to go to school* 4.2
shéi 谁 *who* 1.4
  shéi de 谁的 *whose* 3.2
shénme 什么 *what* 1.4
shēngrì 生日 *birthday* 3.6
shí 十 *ten* 2.2
shì(r) 事（儿）*affair; matter* 4.5
shì 是 *am, are, is* 1.4
  Shì ma? 是吗? *Is that so? is it?* 3.6
shíhou 时候 *time* 4.2
Shǐmìsī 史密斯 *Smith* 1.4
shòu 瘦 *thin* 2.4
shōushi 收拾 *to tidy up* 4.5
shū 书 *book* 3.2
  shūbāo 书包 *schoolbag* 3.1
shuìjiào 睡觉 *to sleep* 4.2
shuō 说 *to say; to speak* 1.3
suì 岁 *years of age* 2.6

T

tā 他 *he; him* 1.4
  tā de 他的 *his* 1.4
  tāmen 他们 *they; them* 1.4
    tāmen de 他们的 *their; theirs* 1.4
tā 她 *she; her* 1.4
tā de 她的 *her, hers* 1.4
tā 它 *it* 2.3
tài … le 太……了 *extremely …; too …* 4.3
tàitai 太太 *Mrs; wife* 2.6
táoqì 淘气 *naughty; mischievous* 2.4
tiān 天 *day; sky; heaven* 3.5
  tiānqì 天气 *weather* 4.5
tiáo 条 *(MW for fish)* 2.3
tīng 听 *to listen* 4.4
tǐng … de 挺……的 *quite …; very …; rather…* 2.4
  tǐng hǎo de 挺好的 *quite good* 1.3
tóngxué 同学 *fellow student* 1.2
  tóngxuémen 同学们 *fellow students* 1.2

W

wǎn 晚 *late* 4.1
  wǎn le 晚了 *to be late* 4.1
  wǎnfàn 晚饭 *evening meal* 4.2
  wǎnshang 晚上 *evening* 4.1
Wáng 王 *(surname)* 2.6
Wáng Hànshēng 王汉生 *(name)* LTR 2.6
  Wáng Huá 王华 *(name)* 3.1
  Wáng Lì 王利 *(name)* LTR 3.2
  Wáng Shū 王书 *(name)* 4.4
  Wáng Yún 王云 *(name)* 4.4
wèi 喂 *hello; hey* 1.3
wèn 问 *to ask* 1.4
wǒ 我 *I; me* 1.4
  wǒ de 我的 *my, mine* 1.4
    wǒ de yì jiā 我的一家 *my family* 2
  wǒmen 我们 *we; us* 1.5
    wǒmen de 我们的 *our, ours* 1.4
wǔ 五 *five* 2.2
wǔfàn 午饭 *lunch* 4.2
wúliáo 无聊 *bored* 4.5

X

Xīní 悉尼 *Sydney* 2.1
xià 下 *to fall (of rain, snow, hail); to leave; next …* 4.5
  xià yǔ 下雨 *to rain* 4.5
  xià gè xīngqī 下个星期 *next week* 3.5
  xià gè yuè 下个月 *next month* 3.5
  xiàkè 下课 *to finish class* 3.3
  xiàwǔ 下午 *afternoon* 4.1
xiānsheng 先生 *Mr; gentleman* 2.6
xiànzài 现在 *now* 4.1
xiàngpí 橡皮 *eraser; rubber* 3.3
xiǎo 小 *small* 2.1
  xiǎo gǒu 小狗 *puppy* 2.4
  xiǎojie 小姐 *Miss; young lady* 2.6
  xiǎo māo 小猫 *kitten* 2.3
  xiǎopéngyou 小朋友 *friendly term of address for child* 2.6
  Xiǎo Míng 小明 *(name)* 4.4
  xiǎoshuō 小说 *novel* 3.4
  xiǎoxué 小学 *primary school* 2.1
xiē 些 *several* 3.4
xiě 写 *write* LTW 1
  xiězài … shàng 写在……上 *to write on (something)* 3.6
xiè 谢 *to thank* 1.3
  xièxie 谢谢 *thank you* 1.3
Xiè Shēngfāng 谢生方 *(name)* LTR 4.2
xìn 信 *letter* 4.4
xīngqī 星期 *week* 3.5
  xīngqī'èr 星期二 *Tuesday* 3.5
  xīngqīliù 星期六 *Saturday* 3.5
  xīngqīsān 星期三 *Wednesday* 3.5
  xīngqīsì 星期四 *Thursday* 3.5
  xīngqītiān 星期天 *Sunday* 3.5
  xīngqīwǔ 星期五 *Friday* 3.5
  xīngqīyī 星期一 *Monday* 3.5
xìng 姓 *surname; to be surnamed* 1.4
xiōngdì jiěmèi 兄弟姐妹 *brothers and sisters* 2.2
xué 学 *to study* 1.5
  xuéhuì 学会 *learn; master* LTR 1.1

xuésheng 学生 *student* 1.4
xuéxiào 学校 *school* 3.1

Y

yáng 羊 *sheep; goat* 2.4
yǎng 养 *to keep, raise* 2.3
yào 要 *to want; to intend* 3.4
yáogǔnyuè 摇滚乐 *rock music* 4.4
yě 也 *also* 1.3
yī 一 *one* 1.3
yìdiǎnr 一点儿 *a little* 4.3
yíhuìr 一会儿 *a short while* 4.4
yì jiā 一家 *(whole) family* 2
yíxià 一下 *(adds informality to tone)* 2.1
yīyuè 一月 *January* 3.5
yīnyuè 音乐 *music* 4.4
Yīngwén 英文 *English language* 3.3
Yīngyǔ 英语 *English language* 3.1
Yīngyǔ lǎoshī 英语老师 *English language teacher* 3.1
yǐwéi 以为 *to think (mistakenly)* 2.4
yǐzi 椅子 *chair* 3.3
yǒu 有 *to have; there is, there are* 2.2
yǒu kòngr 有空儿 *to be free; to have spare time* 4.5
yǒu shíhou 有时候 *sometimes* 4.2
yǒu shìr 有事儿 *to be busy; to have something on* 4.5
yǒu yìsi 有意思 *interesting* 2.4
yóuyǒng 游泳 *to swim* 4.5
yú 鱼 *fish* 2.4
yǔ 雨 *rain* 4.5
yuè 月 *month* 3.5

Z

Zài shuō yí biàn. 再说一遍。*(Please) say it once more.* 3.3
zàijiàn 再见 *goodbye* 1.2
zánmen 咱们 *we; us (includes listener)* 4.1
zǎofàn 早饭 *breakfast* 4.2
zǎoshang 早上 *morning* 4.1
zěnme 怎么 *how* 3.3
zěnmeyàng 怎么样 *how* 4.5
zhāng 张 *(MW for table)* 3.4
Zhāng 张 *(family name)* 1.4
Zhāng Jiàn 张建 *(name)* 4.3
Zhāng Jiànhuá 张建华 *(name)* 1.3
Zhāng Jiànqiū 张建秋 *(name)* 2.1
Zhāng Léi 张雷 *(name)* 2.2
Zhāng Yún 张云 *(name)* 3.4
zhǎo 找 *to look for* 4.4
zhǎo péngyou 找朋友 *to go to see friends* 4.4
Zhào Míng 赵明 *(name)* 2.2
Zhào Qīng 赵青 *(name)* 2.1
Zhào Wén 赵文 *(name)* 2.1
Zhào Yún 赵云 *(name)* 2.1
Zhào Yuǎn 赵远 *(name)* 2.1
zháojí 着急 *to worry, feel anxious* 4.4
zhè 这 *this* 2.1
zhèi 这 *this* 2.4
zhèige xīngqī 这个星期 *this week* 3.5
zhèige yuè 这个月 *this month* 3.5
zhèige 这个 *this (one)* 3.4
zhèixiē 这些 *these (ones)* 3.4
zhēn 真 *really; true* 2.4
Zhēnní 珍妮 *Jenny* 2.1
zhèng(zài) 正(在) *(aspect particle); in the process of* 4.4
zhī 支 *(MW for pencil, pen etc)* 3.2
zhī 只 *(MW for dog, cat etc)* 2.3
zhǐ 只 *only; merely* 2.2
zhǐ yǒu 只有 *only have …* 2.2
zhīdao 知道 *to know* 2.6
Zhōngguó 中国 *China* 1.1
Zhōngguórén 中国人 *Chinese (person)* 1.5
Zhōngwén 中文 *Chinese language* 3.3
zhōngwǔ 中午 *noon, midday* 4.1
zhōngxué 中学 *high school* 2.1
zhù 住 *to live* 2.1
zhù 祝 …… *to wish (someone) …* 3.6
zhuōzi 桌子 *table* 3.1
zì 字 *character; word* LTR 1.1
zìxíngchē 自行车 *bicycle* 3.2
zǒu 走 *to walk; to leave* 4.1
zǒu lù 走路 *to walk* 4.3
zuótiān 昨天 *yesterday* 3.5
zuò 坐 *to sit; to travel by* 1.3
zuò chē 坐车 *to travel by bus, car, train* 4.3
zuò 做 *to do* 4.2
zuò kèjiāncāo 做课间操 *to do set physical exercises* 4.2
zuò zuòyè 做作业 *to do homework* 4.2
zuòyè 作业 *homework* 4.2

Character list 汉字表 (Hànzì biǎo)

(Characters are listed according to number of strokes then in order of their appearance in the Learn to Read sections. Examples given are not intended to be exhaustive.)

		Learn to Write Lesson	Learn to Read Unit/Area
One stroke			
一	yī *one* 星期一	5	2.2
Two strokes			
人	rén *person; people* 中国人	6	1.5
几	jǐ *how many; several* 几个人?	6	2.2
二	èr *two*	5	2.2
七	qī *seven*	5	2.2
八	bā *eight*	5	2.2
九	jiǔ *nine*	5	2.2
十	shí *ten*	5	2.2
了	le *(aspect particle indicating completion or change)* 养了 慢了		2.3
儿	er *(retroflex ending)* 有事儿		4.5
Three strokes			
也	yě *also*	3	1.3
么	me *(as in* shénme*)* 什么 怎么	8	1.4
大	dà *big* 很大 大学 澳大利亚	9	1.5
上	shàng *to attend; preceding, previous; (as in* zǎoshang*); on, up;* 上课 上个星期 上个月 早上	4	2.1
小	xiǎo *small* 小学 小说	7	2.1
个	gè *(measure word)* 几个 两个	6	2.2
三	sān *three*	5	2.2
下	xià *leave; next* 下课 下个月 下个星期 下午	10	3.6

		Learn to Write Lesson	Learn to Read Unit/Area
Four strokes			
见	jiàn *see* 再见		1.2
方	fāng *(as in* Lín Fāng*)* 林方		1.3
什	shén *(as in* shénme*)* 什么	8	1.4
不	bù *not* 不谢 不是 不热 不知道	3	1.5
中	zhōng *middle* 中国 中学 中午	4	1.5
五	wǔ *five*	5	2.2
六	liù *six*	5	2.2
王	wáng *(a surname); king, prince*		2.6
少	shǎo *few, less* 多少？		3.1
文	wén *script; writing; language* 中文		3.3
今	jīn *present* 今天 今年	10	3.5
天	tiān *day; sky; heaven* 今天 天气	10	3.5
日	rì *day* 生日 日本	10	3.6
月	yuè *month* 一月 下个月	10	3.5
午	wǔ *noon, midday* 上午 中午 下午	11	4.1
分	fēn *minute* 十五分	11	4.1
车	chē *vehicle* 自行车 坐车		4.3
书	shū *book* 看书 三本书		4.4
气	qì *air* 天气	14	4.5
Five strokes			
们	men *(pluralising suffix)* 我们 你们 他们	1	1.2
叫	jiào *to be called*	1	1.4
生	shēng *to be born (as in* xuésheng*)* 生日 学生	1	1.4
他	tā *he* 他们	3	1.5
汉	hàn *Han; Chinese* 汉语		1.5

		Learn to Write Lesson	Learn to Read Unit/Area
四	sì *four*	5	2.2
兄	xiōng *elder brother* 兄弟		2.2
只	zhī *(measure word)* 一只猫		2.3
	zhǐ *only; merely* 只有		
北	běi *north* 北京		2.6
对	duì *right, correct; towards, to* 对了 对不起		2.6
本	běn *(measure word); book* 一本书 课本 日本		3.3
可	kě *(used for emphasis); can, may* 可好看了		3.4
号	hào *number; date* 几号?	10	3.5
乐	lè *happy* 快乐		3.6
半	bàn *half* 十二点半	11	4.1
业	yè *(as in* zuòyè*)* 作业		4.2
正	zhèng *(aspect particle indicating an action in progress)* 正在		4.4
去	qù *to go; last (as in* qùnián*)* 去打球 去年		4.5
打	dǎ *to strike; to play (ball-games)* 打球		4.5

Six strokes

		Learn to Write Lesson	Learn to Read Unit/Area
老	lǎo *old; (as in* lǎoshī*)* 老师	1	1.2
师	shī *teacher* 老师	1	1.2
好	hǎo *good; well* 你好！ 你好吗？ 挺好的	1	1.2
再	zài *again* 再见		1.2
吗	ma *(question particle)*	9	1.3
名	míng *name* 名字	8	1.4
字	zì *character, word, letter* 名字	8	1.4
她	tā *she, her* 她们	3	1.5
亚	yà *(as in* Àodàliyà*)* 澳大利亚		1.5
那	nà *that* 那是……	9	2.1

		Learn to Write Lesson	Learn to Read Unit/Area
	nèi *that* 那个 那只猫		
妈	mā *mother* 妈妈	4	2.1
有	yǒu *to have* 我有一个姐姐。有事儿	6	2.2
同	tóng *same; together with* 同学们		2.6
岁	suì *years old, age* 几岁？十二岁	7	2.6
多	duō *many* 多少？很多		3.1
问	wèn *to ask* 请问，……		3.2
年	nián *year* 今年 明年 哪年？	10	3.5
在	zài *at; on; (as in* zhèngzài*)* 正在	11	4.1
早	zǎo *early* 早上 早饭	12	4.2
吃	chī *to eat* 吃午饭		4.2
回	huí *to return* 回家	13	4.2
自	zì *self* 自行车		4.3
行	xíng *walk, travel, move* 自行车		4.3

Seven strokes

你	nǐ *you (singular)* 你们	1	1.2
我	wǒ *I; me* 我们 我的	1	1.4
利	lì *(as in* Àodàlìyà*)* 澳大利亚		1.5
这	zhè *this* 这是……	4	2.1
	zhèi *this* 这个 这只狗		
两	liǎng *two (of something)* 两个弟弟 两只猫		2.2
没	méi *not* 没有	7	2.2
弟	dì *younger brother* 弟弟 兄弟姐妹	7	2.2
进	jìn *to enter* 请进！		2.4
住	zhù *to live* 他住哪儿？	7	2.6

		Learn to Write Lesson	Learn to Read Unit/Area
还	hái *still, also; (as in* háishi*)* 还有 还是		2.6
快	kuài *happy; soon* 生日快乐！ 快七岁了		3.6
每	měi *every* 每天		4.2
床	chuáng *bed* 起床	12	4.2
饭	fàn *meal* 吃午饭		4.2
作	zuò *to do, act, compose, write* 作业		4.2
走	zǒu *to walk* 走路		4.3
坐	zuò *to sit; to travel by …* 坐车		4.3
冷	lěng *cold* 怕冷	14	4.5

Eight strokes

的	de *(structural particle)* 我的 你的	4	1.3
呢	ne *(sentence particle)* 你呢？	8	1.3
林	lín *(a surname); forest* 林方		1.3
学	xué *to learn* 学生 学汉语 中学 学校	1	1.4
国	guó *country* 中国 哪国人？		1.5
爸	bà *father* 爸爸	4	2.1
妹	mèi *younger sister* 妹妹 兄弟姐妹	6	2.1
姐	jiě *elder sister* 姐姐	7	2.2
和	hé *and, with* 弟弟和妹妹	6	2.2
狗	gǒu *dog* 一只狗		2.3
京	jīng *capital* 北京		2.6
知	zhī *to know* 知道		3.1
明	míng *bright, clear* 明天 明年 小明	10	3.6
现	xiàn *now* 现在	11	4.1
表	biǎo *watch (timepiece)*		4.1
放	fàng *to let go, release* 放学	13	4.2

Learn to Write Lesson	Learn to Read Unit/Area
怕	pà	*to fear, be afraid of*	怕冷　怕热		4.5
事	shì	*affair, business*	有事儿		4.5

Nine strokes

挺	tǐng	*rather, quite; very*	挺好的		1.3
是	shì	*am, is, are*	我是学生。	2	1.4
语	yǔ	*language*	汉语		1.5
养	yǎng	*to raise, keep*	养狗　养猫		2.3
哪	nǎ	*where*	住哪（儿）？		
	něi	*which*	哪个？　哪国人？	8	3.1
很	hěn	*very*	很好　很大	9	3.1
给	gěi	*to give; to*	给你　借给		3.2
怎	zěn	*how*	怎么？		3.3
说	shuō	*to say*	怎么说？　说汉语　小说		3.3
看	kàn	*to look, watch, read*	看书　好看		2.4
要	yào	*to want*	我要这本。		3.4
星	xīng	*star*	星期	10	3.5
祝	zhù	*to express good wishes*	祝你生日快乐！		3.6
点	diǎn	*o'clock*	三点半	11	4.1
觉	jiào	*sleep*	睡觉	13	4.2
昨	zuó	*yesterday*	昨天		4.4
咱	zán	*we (including the listener)*	咱们		4.5
帮	bāng	*to help*	帮我……		4.5

Ten strokes

哥	gē	*elder brother*	哥哥	7	2.2
家	jiā	*home; family*	我的家	6	2.3
请	qǐng	*request, ask; please*	请进！		2.4
谁	shéi	*who*	谁的？	9	2.4

				Learn to Write Lesson	Learn to Read Unit/Area
真	zhēn	*real, true; genuine*	真好看		2.4
校	xiào	*school*	学校	9	3.1
笔	bǐ	*writing implement*			3.2
课	kè	*lesson*	课本 上课 下课		3.3
借	jiè	*to borrow, lend*	借给		3.4
起	qǐ	*to rise, get up*	起床	12	4.2
赶	gǎn	*catch up with; rush through*	赶作业		4.4
热	rè	*hot*	天气很热 怕热	14	4.5
Eleven strokes					
猫	māo	*cat*	一只猫 养猫		2.3
做	zuò	*to do, make*	做作业		4.2
球	qiú	*ball*	打球		4.5
Twelve strokes					
道	dào	*way*	知道		3.1
谢	xiè	*to thank*	谢谢 不谢		3.2
期	qī	*period of time*	星期四	10	3.5
晚	wǎn	*evening, night; late, to be late*	晚上 晚了	13	4.2
Thirteen strokes					
睡	shuì	*to sleep*	睡觉	13	4.2
路	lù	*road, way*	走路		4.3
Fourteen strokes					
慢	màn	*slow*	表慢了		4.1
Fifteen strokes					
懂	dǒng	*to understand*	懂了		3.3
Sixteen strokes					
澳	ào	*(as in Àodàlìyà)*	澳大利亚		1.5

Index to grammar and usage references

Vocabulary reference

Transliterations of common English names

Adam	Yàdāng	亚当
Adrian	Àidélǐ' ān	艾德里安
Alan	Ālún	阿伦
Alex	Yàlìkèsī	亚历克斯
Alison	Ālìsēn	阿莉森
Andrew	Āndélǔ	安德鲁
Angela	Ānjílā	安吉拉
Ann	Ān	安
Annette	Ānnítè	安妮特
Anthony	Āndōngní	安东尼
Arthur	Yàsè	亚瑟
Audrey	Àodélì	奥德丽
Barbara	Bābālā	巴巴拉
Barry	Bālǐ	巴里
Belinda	Bǐlíndá	比琳达
Ben	Běn	本
Bernadette	Bónàdàitè	伯纳黛特
Bernard	Bónàdé	伯纳德
Beth	Bèisī	贝思
Betty	Bèidì	贝蒂
Bill	Bǐ'ěr	比尔
Bob	Bàobó	鲍勃
Brenda	Bùlúndá	布伦达
Brian	Bùlài'ēn	布赖恩
Bridget	Bùlìqítè	布丽奇特
Bruce	Bùlǔsī	布鲁斯
Carol	Kǎluó'ěr	卡罗尔
Caroline	Kǎluólín	卡罗琳
Cathy	Kǎixī	凯茜
Charlie	Chálì	查利
Christine	Kèlǐsītíng	克里斯廷
Chris	Kèlǐsī	克里斯
Clive	Kèláifū	克莱夫
Colin	Kēlín	科林
Connie	Kāngnī	康妮
Cynthia	Xīnxīyà	辛西娅
Dan	Dān	丹
Daphne	Dáfūnī	达夫妮
David	Dàwèi	大卫
Deborah	Dàibólā	黛博拉
Denise	Dānnīsī	丹妮斯
Denis	Dānnísī	丹尼斯
Derek	Délǐkè	德里克
Des	Désī	德斯
Diana	Dài'ānnà	黛安娜
Dick	Díkè	迪克
Donna	Tángnà	唐娜
Don	Táng	唐
Dorothy	Duōlèxī	多勒西
Douglas	Dàogélāsī	道格拉斯
Duncan	Dèngkěn	邓肯
Edith	Yīdísī	伊迪丝
Eileen	Àilín	艾琳
Elizabeth	Yīlìshābái	伊丽莎白
Ellen	Āilún	埃伦
Elsie	Āi'ěrxī	埃尔西
Emily	Āimǐlì	埃米莉
Eric	Āilǐkè	埃里克
Eva	Yīwá	伊娃
Evelyn	Yīfūlín	伊夫林
Fay	Fèiyī	费伊
Frank	Fúlánkè	弗兰克
Fred	Fúléidé	弗雷德
Gary	Jiālǐ	加里
Gay	Gàiyī	盖伊
Gerry	Gélǐ	格里
Geoff	Jiéfú	杰弗
Gladys	Gélādísī	格拉迪斯
Glynn	Gélín	格林
Gordon	Gēdēng	戈登
Graham	Géléi'èmǔ	格雷厄姆
Grant	Gélántè	格兰特
Gregory	Géléigēlǐ	格雷戈里
Guy	Gàiyī	盖伊
Hugh	Hālǐ	哈里
Harvey	Hāwéi	哈维
Helen	Hǎilún	海伦
Hilary	Sīlālǐ	希拉里
Howard	Huòhuádé	霍华德
Harry	xiū	休
Ian	Yī'ēn	伊恩
Isabel	Yīshābèi'ěr	伊莎贝尔
Jack	Jiékè	杰克
Jane	Jiǎn	简
Janet	Zhēnnītè	珍妮特
Jean	Jí'ēn	吉恩
Jenny	Zhānnī	詹妮
Jeremy	Jiélǐmǐ	杰里米
Jim	Jímǔ	吉姆
Joan	Qióng	琼
John	Yuēhàn	约翰
Joy	Qiáoyī	乔伊
Judith	Zhūdísī	朱迪思
Julia	Zhūlìyà	朱莉娅
Justin	Jiǎsītíng	贾斯廷
Kate	Kǎitè	凯特
Kathleen	Kǎisīlín	凯思琳
Kay	Kǎi	凯
Keith	Jīsī	基思
Ken	Kěn	肯
Kerry	Kèlǐ	克里
Larry	Lālǐ	拉里
Laura	Láolā	劳拉

Laurie	Láolǐ	劳里
Lesley	Láisīlì	莱斯莉
Linda	Líndá	琳达
Lindsay	Línsài	林赛
Louise	Lùyìsī	路易丝
Lucy	Lùxī	露西
Lydia	Lìdíyà	莉迪亚
Lynn	Lín'ēn	林恩
Margaret	Mǎgélìtè	玛格丽特
Margot	Mǎgē	玛戈
Marian	Mǎlì'ān	玛丽安
Marie	Mǎlì	玛丽
Mark	Mǎkè	马克
Martin	Mǎdīng	马丁
Mary	Mǎlì	玛丽
Maryann	Mǎlì'ān	玛丽安
Matthew	Mǎxiū	马修
Maurice	Mòlǐsī	莫里斯
Max	Mǎkèsī	马克斯
Mike	Màikè	迈克
Monica	Méngnīkǎ	蒙妮卡
Nancy	Nánxī	南希
Natalie	Nàtǎlì	纳塔莉
Neil	Ní'ěr	尼尔
Neville	Nèiwéi'ěr	内维尔
Nick	Níkè	尼克
Nigel	Nàijié'ěr	奈杰尔
Noel	Nuòāi'ěr	诺埃尔
Nola	Nuòlā	诺拉
Owen	Ōuwén	欧文
Pamela	Pàméilā	帕梅拉
Pat	Pàtè	帕特
Paul	Bǎoluó	保罗
Paula	Bōlā	波拉
Peter	Bǐdé	彼得
Philip	Fēilìpǔ	菲利普（菲力普）
Polly	Bōlì	波莉
Rachel	Léiqiè'ěr	雷切尔
Ralph	Lā'ěrfū	拉尔夫
Reg	Léijí	雷吉
Robin	Luóbīn	罗宾
Roger	Luójié	罗杰
Ron	Láng	朗
Ross	Luósī	罗斯
Roy	Luóyī	罗伊
Russell	Luósù	罗素
Ruth	Lǔsī	鲁思
Sally	Sàlì	萨莉
Sam	Sàmǔ	萨姆
Sandra	Sāngdélā	桑德拉
Sean	Xiāoēn	肖恩
Shelley	Xièlì	谢利（谢莉）
Shirley	Xuělì	雪利（雪莉）
Simon	Xīméng	西蒙
Sonia	Suǒníyà	索尼娅
Steve	Shǐdìfū	史蒂夫
Stuart	Sītúěrtè	斯图尔特
Sue	Sū	苏
Tanya	Tǎníyà	塔尼娅
Ted	Tèdé	特德
Terry	Tèlǐ	特里
Tim	Dìmǔ	蒂姆
Toby	Tuōbǐ	托比
Tom	Tāngmǔ	汤姆
Tony	Tuōní	托尼
Tracy	Tèlèixī	特蕾西
Veronica	Wéilángnīkǎ	维朗妮卡
Vicki	Wéijī	维基
Wally	Wòlì	沃利
Wendy	Wēndí	温迪
Yvonne	Yīféng	伊冯
Zoe	Zuǒyī	佐伊

Classroom phrases

上课！ Shàngkè! *Let's begin!*

起立！ Qǐlì! *Rise! (said by class monitor when teacher comes in and before the teacher leaves)*

坐下！ Zuòxia! *Be seated.*

报告！ Bàogào! *Reporting! (said when you are late, outside the door)*

进来！ Jìnlai! *Come in!*

请打开书。 Qǐng dǎkāi shū. *Please open your books.*

请看黑板(写字板)。 Qǐng kàn hēibǎn (or xiězìbǎn). *Please look at the blackboard (or board).*

请你念。 Qǐng nǐ niàn. *Please read out aloud.*

我念。 Wǒ niàn. *I'll read.*

你们听。 Nǐmen tīng. *You listen.*

跟我念。 Gēn wǒ niàn. *Read after me.*

快一点儿。 Kuài yìdiǎnr. *Hurry up.*

我问。 Wǒ wèn. *I'll ask questions.*

你们回答。 Nǐmen huídá. *You answer.*

你说。 Nǐ shuō. *You say it.*

再说一遍。 Zài shuō yí biàn. *Repeat.*

对。 Duì. *That's right*

不对。 Bú duì. *That's wrong.*

一个一个说。 Yí gè yí gè shuō. *Say it one by one.*

一个一个来 Yí gè yí gè lái. *(Do it) one by one.*

注意听。 Zhùyì tīng. *Listen carefully.*

注意发音。 Zhùyì fāyīn. *Pay attention to your pronunciation.*

注意声调。 Zhùyì shēngdiào. *Pay attention to your tones.*

你懂了吗？ Nǐ dǒng le ma? *Do you understand?*

你听懂了吗？ Nǐ tīngdǒng le ma? *Did you understand (through listening)?*

我不懂。 Wǒ bù dǒng. *I don't understand.*

我还不懂。 Wǒ hái bù dǒng. *I still don't understand.*

举手！ Jǔ shǒu! *Put you hands up!*

（请）排好队。 (Qǐng) páihǎo duì. *Please line up.*

请你站起来。 Qǐng nǐ zhàn qilai. *Please stand up.*

请安静一点儿！ Qǐng ānjìng yìdiǎnr! *Please be a bit quieter!*

不要说话！ Búyào shuōhuà! *Don't talk!*

下课！ Xiàkè! *Class dismissed!*

Pronunciation and spelling rules

What are tones

1. Chinese is a tonal language in which every syllable has its specific tone. A change of tone involves a change of meaning.

e.g.	*qìchē* – car	*qí chē* – to ride a bicycle
	hǎo – good	*hào* – number
	dà – big	*dǎ* – to play (ball games)

2. In Standard Chinese (or *pǔtōnghuà*) there are four basic tones represented by the following tone marks:

	1st tone	2nd tone	3rd tone	4th tone
e.g.	tā	tóngxué	wǒ	zàijiàn

3. When speaking there are also syllables which are unstressed and take a feeble tone. This is known as the neutral tone and is represented by the tone mark '°'. Usually this tone mark is left out.

   e.g. *Nǐ nȇ?* or Nǐ ne?

Tone marks

1. In the official *pīnyīn* system of romanisation the tone mark is always placed over a vowel (e.g. *nǐ, wǒ, tā*).
2. If the syllable contains three vowels (e.g. *xiǎo*), the tone mark is placed over the middle vowel.
3. If the syllable contains two vowels, the tone mark is written over the first vowel (e.g. *hǎo, zài*) unless the first vowel is an *i* or a *u*, in which case it is written over the second vowel (e.g. *xièxie, xuésheng*).
4. When a tone mark is placed over an 'i', the dot over the "i" is dropped.

Tone changes

Sometimes tones are affected by other tones.

1. One example is the 3rd tone. When two or more 3rd tones immediately follow each other, only the **last** one is pronounced in the 3rd tone, the preceding ones are pronounced as 2nd tones

   e.g. *Nǐ hǎo!* is pronounced *Ní hǎo!*

   (Note that *Nǐmen hǎo* is still pronounced as *Nǐmen hǎo* because the suffix -men comes between the two 3rd tone syllables *nǐ* and *hǎo*.)

2. When a 3rd tone is followed by a 1st, 2nd or 4th tone or most neutral tones, it usually becomes a half-third tone, i.e. the tone only falls but does not rise. Note that when a 3rd tone is pronounced as a half-third tone its tone mark remains unchanged.

   e.g. *xiǎoshuō* *dǎ qiú* *kě'ài* *nǚde*

3. Another word which changes its tone is *bù*. When *bù* is followed by a 4th tone (or a neutral tone that was originally a 4th tone), it is pronounced in the 2nd tone.

   e.g. *bú shì*
   bú tài gāo
   bú duì

4 The number *yī* is pronounced in the 1st tone when standing by itself. When it is followed by another syllable it changes its tone.

Yī	**followed by**	**changes into**	**example**
	4th tone or neutral tone	2nd tone	*yí liàng qìchē* *yí gè xuésheng*
	all other tones	4th tone	*yì zhī māo* *yì běn shū*

Rules of phonetic spelling

1. When a syllable beginning with *a, o* or *e* follows another syllable in such a way that the division of the two syllables could be confused, an apostrophe is put in to mark the division clearly to avoid ambiguity.

   e.g. *kě'ài shí'èr*

2. At the beginning of a syllable, *i* is written as *y*.

   e.g. *ie – ye*
   ian – yan

   I is written as *yi* when it forms a syllable by itself.

3. At the beginning of a syllable, *u* is written as *w*.

   e.g. *uo –wo*

   U is written as *wu* when it forms a syllable by itself.

4. When forming syllables by themselves, *in* and *ing* are written as *yin* and *ying* respectively.

5. When *ü* and the finals* that begin with *ü* appear after *j, q* or *x, ü* is written as *u*, with the umlaut omitted.

   e.g. *xuésheng*

Stress

Pŭtōnghuà or standard Chinese distinguishes roughly three degrees of stress of polysyllabic words: main (or strong) stress, medium stress, and weak stress.

1. In most disyllabic words, the strong stress falls on the second syllable, and the first syllable is usually pronounced with a medium stress.

   e.g. *Hànyǔ lǎoshī zàijiàn dǎ qiú qìchē diànshì*

2. Most words of three syllables have a main stress falling on the last syllable. The usual stress pattern is 'medium – weak – strong'.

   e.g. *túshūguǎn Zhōngguórén zìxíngchē pīngpāngqiú*

* A Chinese syllable is usually made up of an initial (the beginning consonant) and a final (a vowel, a compound vowel or a vowel plus a nasal consonant).

e.g. *mā hǎo běn*
m, h and *b* are the initials,
a, ao and *en* are the finals